Exploring Utah's Bears Ears and Cedar Mesa

Help Us Keep This Guide Up to Date

Every effort has been made by the author and editors to make this guide as accurate and useful as possible. However, many things can change after a guide is published—trails are rerouted, regulations change, techniques evolve, facilities come under new management, etc.

We appreciate hearing from you concerning your experiences with this guide and how you feel it could be improved and kept up to date. While we may not be able to respond to all comments and suggestions, we'll take them to heart and we'll also make certain to share them with the author. Please send your comments and suggestions to the following address:

FalconGuides
Reader Response/Editorial Department
246 Goose Lane, Suite 200
Guilford, CT 06437

Thanks for your input, and happy trails!

Front cover photo: Nevills Arch in Owl Canyon. Back cover photo: Comb Ridge and the Abajo Mountains above the San Juan River corridor.

Exploring Utah's Bears Ears and Cedar Mesa

A Guide to Hiking, Backpacking, Scenic Drives, and Landmarks

Andrew Weber

GUILFORD, CONNECTICUT

To Heather, Bennett, and Russell, who kept the home fires burning.

FALCONGUIDES®

An imprint of The Rowman & Littlefield Publishing Group, Inc.
4501 Forbes Blvd., Ste. 200
Lanham, MD 20706
www.rowman.com

Falcon and FalconGuides are registered trademarks and Make Adventure Your Story is a trademark of The Rowman & Littlefield Publishing Group, Inc.

Distributed by NATIONAL BOOK NETWORK

Photos by Andrew Weber unless otherwise noted
Maps by The Rowman & Littlefield Publishing Group, Inc.

British Library Cataloguing in Publication Information available

Library of Congress Cataloging-in-Publication Data

Names: Weber, Andrew, 1971- author.
Title: Exploring Utah's Bears Ears and Cedar Mesa : a guide to hiking, backpacking, scenic drives, and landmarks / Andrew Weber.
Description: Guilford, Connecticut : FalconGuides, [2021] | Series: Exploring series
Identifiers: LCCN 2020054026 (print) | LCCN 2020054027 (ebook) | ISBN 9781493046188 (paperback) | ISBN 9781493046195 (epub)
Subjects: LCSH: Hiking—Utah—San Juan County—Guidebooks. | National monuments—Utah—Guidebooks. | Hiking—Bears Ears National Monument (Utah)—Guidebooks. | Backpacking—Bears Ears National Monument (Utah)—Guidebooks. | Bears Ears National Monument (Utah)—Guidebooks. | Cedar Mesa (San Juan County, Utah)—Guidebooks.
Classification: LCC GV199.42.U82 S258 2021 (print) | LCC GV199.42.U82 (ebook) | DDC 796.5109792/59--dc23
LC record available at https: // lccn.loc.gov/2020054026
LC ebook record available at https: // lccn.loc.gov/2020054027

♾️™ The paper used in this publication meets the minimum requirements of American National Standard for Information Sciences—Permanence of Paper for Printed Library Materials, ANSI/NISO Z39.48-1992.

Contents

Foreword

I still vividly remember the first few days my wife and I spent in Bears Ears National Monument. We went for a hike up the South Fork of Mule Canyon on Cedar Mesa and snapped photos of the House on Fire granaries. We also explored Arch and Owl Canyons. We had the place to ourselves, not seeing another visitor in three days. It was a life-changing weekend that eventually resulted in us moving to Bluff, Utah, and my taking the job as executive director of Friends of Cedar Mesa.

That was in 2001, when the area wasn't yet known as Bears Ears. In those days, before the advent of Facebook or Instagram, visitors had just begun to "discover" the remarkable archaeology, geology, and scenery of the area. Of course, the cultural richness of the area had been known to experts for many years. As far back as 1904, Southwestern archaeologist Edgar Lee Hewett submitted a report to Congress calling for the area to be protected in response to what was already an extensive history of looting. And it's worth explicitly acknowledging that long before Anglo explorers showed up, indigenous peoples lived throughout this sacred landscape where the spirits of their ancestors reside, as still celebrated in their oral traditions today.

Now, two decades later, the cat is out of the bag; you're very unlikely to walk up to House on Fire and not see another group of hikers. The skyrocketing visitation to Bears Ears is due largely to the advent of social media, which has "blown up" with images of the area's iconic beauty and intriguing cultural sites. There's no viewing a photo of one of the iconic cliff dwellings of Bears Ears and not saying to yourself, "I gotta see that one day."

Increased visitation isn't just due to the internet. No national monument in modern history has received more media attention, which sprang from the controversy over the monument's creation in 2016 by President Obama at the request of a coalition of Native American tribes and pueblos. Even more controversy resulted from the reduction of the monument by President Trump in 2017, a move whose legality is still under dispute and may eventually be decided by the US Supreme Court.

If you've bought this book, you're probably headed to Bears Ears, so I'll let the land speak for itself when you see it. I'll hazard a guess that you'll agree with me it deserves to be protected forever, as intended by the original monument designation.

But whatever your opinion on the size and status of the monument, I think we can all agree that these ancestral territories that are now managed as public lands—containing more than 100,000 archaeological sites—should be visited with respect.

While it may seem like the Wild West—lacking the signs, rangers, and crowds of America's national parks—Bears Ears is not a playground. Rather, it's a living cultural landscape that is sacred to the indigenous peoples who once called this area home and still live nearby today. What might look like a photogenic cliff dwelling or petroglyph to you is actually a spiritual place for Native American descendants of the people who made these sites. The least we can do to acknowledge the sacred nature of this area is to tread softly, speak quietly, leave as little impact as we can, and follow the Visit with Respect tips you'll read about in this book.

I have to admit that when FalconGuides first approached Friends of Cedar Mesa about partnering on a guidebook, we had some trepidation about the idea. Previous guidebooks have not been good for this area, and some authors have directed visitors to places too sensitive to handle mass visitation. Yet we knew that visitors need good information to have an inspirational experience, be safe, and have minimal impact on this internationally significant area.

To their credit, Falcon reassured us they wanted to make a responsible guide that would teach people how to visit respectfully. They asked us for advice on who should write the book, collaborated with us on the selection of sites to include, and featured the principles of our Visit with Respect program throughout the text. This guide is the end result, the best and most responsible guidebook available to the area, well worth your investment.

Far from a tourist-turned-guidebook-writer, author Andrew Weber has served as a long-term volunteer at Cedar Mesa and makes the Four Corners his permanent home. He cares deeply about the future of Bears Ears and takes seriously his responsibility as someone directing people through this sensitive landscape. The results of his hard work will give you many productive and inspiring days of exploring. Should you elect to venture beyond the sites he has outlined here, you'll have learned key tips of how to visit appropriately, showing respect for those who came before you and those who will follow generations from now.

Here's to walking softly and visiting with respect!

—Josh Ewing, Executive Director, Friends of Cedar Mesa

Preface

Look at a map of southeast Utah; a funny thing will happen. Maybe you will notice how large Bears Ears is. Maybe you will notice how small it is. Or maybe you won't be able to find it at all.

A lot depends on when your map was produced—and whether you even know what you're looking for. Prior to 2016, "Bears Ears" referred only to a pair of 9,000-foot buttes of little interest to the outside world. Unless you happened to be looking at a USGS topographic map, they were probably unmarked.

All that changed at the end of President Obama's second term. As one of his last legislative acts, Obama created Bears Ears National Monument

Rain on the Bears Ears Buttes.

at the urging of a coalition of Native American groups. No sooner had Trump taken office than he reversed that action and reduced the monument by more than 80 percent. The result was confusion on the ground and a host of still-unresolved lawsuits. Maps drawn during this tumultuous period might show either the large original monument or its later, shrunken remnants.

The legal and political controversy brought a lot of national attention to Bears Ears—and another layer of confusion. Debates about what Bears Ears might be in the future were clouded by an inability to define exactly what it was in the present. A pair of buttes? The original monument? The reduced monument?

The term "Bears Ears" has now come to refer to the entire landscape. This is the most common current usage; when someone says they are "heading to Bears Ears," they mean they are headed out into this broad region rather than to any specific place within it. This is similar to how people say they live in "Four Corners" or "the Southwest."

The defining element of Bears Ears is its cultural history. For thousands of years, people lived and traveled throughout the region, most notably the Ancestral Puebloans, whose ancient structures and rock art still animate the land. Their range was huge, reflected in the size and scope of the area today. It encompasses mountains, canyons, mesas, buttes, forests, and deserts, with more than a mile of vertical distance between its lowest and highest points, and stretches roughly from the San Juan River in the south to the edge of Canyonlands National Park in the north and the town of Blanding in the east to the shores of Lake Powell in the west.

At well over 2,000 square miles, Bears Ears is substantially larger than all of Utah's "Mighty Five" national parks (Arches, Bryce, Capitol Reef, Canyonlands, and Zion)–*combined*. It's a lot to take in. You could spend a lifetime and not see it all. I should know; I've spent more than twenty years exploring it and I'm not finished yet.

Even for an experienced visitor, the scale can be overwhelming. How do you get a handle on something as vast and varied as Bears Ears? Where does a person begin?

The answer is, you begin right here. You begin with this book.

Introduction

You never forget your first time in a Cedar Mesa canyon. For me, it came in the fall of 2001, just after the events of 9/11. I had come with a friend from Seattle, and before the trip was finished we vowed to return every year, despite the distance and whatever difficulties might arise.

We didn't quite live up to that vow, but no matter. Why visit just once a year? By the end of the decade I had upended my life to move to Four Corners and become a ranger at Kane Gulch. I've spent countless days exploring the landscape ever since.

I'd been around the world and seen many things, but there was something in those canyons that I hadn't found anywhere else. More than in any other place I've been before or since, I experienced something rare and precious: *the thrill of discovery*. That's what this book can provide.

It's an unlikely promise for a guidebook to make—how can this book, widely available to the public, lead to anything "undiscovered"? Yet I believe this promise can be kept.

Even as visitation grows at Bears Ears, year after year, there are still opportunities to feel the same thrill I did back in 2001. Reach every destination in the book and I guarantee you will see many things you have never seen before—and at least one thing that seems like you are the first person to see it, ever.

Find a cliff dwelling in a secluded canyon and you will experience an immediate connection to the past, beyond what a thousand artifacts in a museum could ever provide. Gaze in quiet wonder at the worn grooves of the grinding stones, the individual finger impressions in the mortar, the charcoal-stained wall where cooking fires once blazed. It will seem like the people who built the structure are close enough to touch, even though they left around 1300 CE. It will also feel like no one else has been there since.

That is the magic of Bears Ears. And just like the kind performed by magicians on a stage, it is not anything supernatural, but instead an elaborate illusion.

The thrill comes from *feeling* like you are the first person to arrive in seven centuries, even if in reality you are not the first person that month, that week, or even that day. If any previous visitor left some intrusive mark of their passing, the spell will be broken. The same goes for you: What you do affects everyone who comes after.

Deep in a Cedar Mesa canyon I once found a perforated seashell fragment, an apparent necklace pendant. Extensive trading networks used by the Ancestral Puebloans linked this part of Utah with civilizations as far away as Central America. This shell must have been sourced through one of these networks, probably from the Pacific Ocean or the Gulf of Mexico, and been an item of considerable rarity and value to the ancients.

The temptation to slip it into my pocket and create a one-of-a-kind souvenir was hard to resist. But just as I would not walk into one of the great cathedrals of Europe and make off with a piece from the altar, so it was with this pendant. Instead, I admired it, wondered about its provenance, and then left it for the next would-be discoverer to unearth anew. I didn't get a souvenir, but I did get something better: the thrill of finding a rare artifact in the wild. The pendant can only be turned into a souvenir once, but it can provide the same thrill over and over to anyone who stumbles across it—as long as they leave it in place.

Ancient petroglyph boulder.

This guidebook will not tell you how to find that pendant, but it will lead you to places where you might make a similar discovery. It provides chapters on thirty-two separate destinations—a mix of hikes, backpacks, scenic drives, and drivable landmarks—with detailed descriptions on how to get there and what you will see when you do. The introduction adds background material on the physical environment, archaeological resources, weather and climate, required permits, and more. Look in the back of the book for a glossary of terms, a list of sources for further reading and reference, and general information for any trip you might take in Bears Ears, including potential hazards.

Regardless of whether you are lucky enough to find an artifact like the pendant, however, you are sure to encounter cultural and archaeological sites everywhere you go. This book provides information on responsible behavior for when you do, through a program called Visit with Respect. Read the program's overview later in the Introduction, and then look for featured icons throughout the text highlighting particular practices in the places they are needed most. Armed with the ethos of Visit with Respect, you will be ready for any experience across the landscape.

Follow this book's lead, and the magic of Bears Ears can be maintained long into the future. If everyone acts responsibly, the thrill of discovery that has meant so much to me—and, hopefully, you, after using this guide—can be maintained forever. That thrill is an infinitely renewable resource, but only if we work to keep it. I hope this book shows you the way.

Weather and Climate

The high season for visiting Bears Ears is the spring and fall. Warm days and cool nights provide ideal conditions for exploring the landscape, and most of the time the weather is pleasant.

Spring is the most popular time to visit, especially for heading out on the trails. From late March to mid-May, temperatures tend to be ideal for hiking, and the melting snowpack generally means most water sources are full. The plentiful moisture causes plants to awaken and bloom.

Daytime highs are generally in the 70s and 80s, and although frost at night is not uncommon, temperatures rarely dip much below freezing.

However, spring weather can be unstable. Late winter storms can blow in at any time, bringing stark temperature drops, sustained rainfall, and sometimes even snow. Howling winds can bring dust storms up from the

Storm clouds rising over Kane Gulch.

low desert, leaving anyone exposed feeling as though they were facing a sandblaster.

It doesn't take much precipitation to render most of the dirt roads in the area impassable, always an issue after a spring rain. Roads in the high alpine country on Elk Ridge may also be snowbound, and in exceptional years they may not melt out until June.

The fall has a similar temperature profile to the spring, making for another season of mild days and an ideal time for exploring the backcountry.

Water sources in the fall, however, can be unreliable. In some years, summer monsoons bring plenty of precipitation to replenish the springs. In other years, the monsoons fail and the heat of summer leaves most water sources dried out.

In general, the weather is quite stable in the fall, with sustained periods of sun and warmth. Many Ancestral Puebloan ruins are at their most evocative in late September and October, when they are bathed with the golden light of autumn. The changing leaves of the aspens in alpine regions and the cottonwoods in the canyon bottoms bring a mix of oranges, yellows, and reds to the landscape.

Summers can be brutally hot, with peak daytime temperatures topping triple digits and no shade to be found. Few people will want to spend much time in the backcountry during this season. If you do intend to venture out on the trails, the best plan is to start as early as possible—at dawn, if you can—and be finished by lunchtime. Keeping trips short is the way to go.

The summer is good for activities that don't require too much time out in the open, like taking scenic drives and visiting drivable landmarks. These allow you to remain sheltered in your air-conditioned vehicle as much as possible.

As for most of the desert Southwest, July and August bring summer monsoons. Clouds pile up throughout the day and turn into thunderstorms in the afternoon. The dark thunderheads can make for dramatic displays over the buttes and mesas, complete with rainbows, lightning, and hail. Sometimes the wrath of nature can be observed from afar, but getting caught underneath one of these thunderstorms is no picnic. The storms can release a Pandora's box of hazards, including flash floods in the canyons and washed-out roads on the mesa tops.

Winter is the least popular time to visit Bears Ears, and for good reason. Although there are some warm and sunny periods, freezing temperatures and cold winds are common. Snowstorms blanket the region, sometimes lasting for days, and the snowpack leaves most areas unreachable behind blocked roads, especially in the high alpine region.

Accordingly, visitors during the winter will likely have a lot of difficulty reaching many popular destinations—but they will also tend to have the place entirely to themselves if they make the trip. Less-hardy souls don't arrive until the spring thaw.

The chart below shows average monthly high and low temperatures and precipitation totals near the towns of Bluff and Blanding, Utah, at an elevation of approximately 5,000 feet.

	Jan	Feb	Mar	Apr	May	Jun	Jul	Aug	Sep	Oct	Nov	Dec
Avg. high temp (°F)	43	50	60	71	79	89	94	91	83	69	55	44
Avg. low temp (°F)	21	26	32	38	47	55	62	61	52	40	29	22
Avg. rainfall (inches)	1.13	.97	.82	.72	.63	.61	1.00	1.11	1.21	1.13	.89	.92

Note that changes in elevation can have significant effects on both temperatures and rainfall amounts. Temperatures at the lowest parts of Bears Ears along the San Juan River (about 4,000 feet) are often 5 to 10 degrees warmer than shown here. Bears Ears Buttes and Elk Ridge (about 8,500 feet) can often be 10 to 15 degrees cooler. Most of Cedar Mesa lies above 6,000 feet, meaning slightly lower temperatures can be expected.

Precipitation shows similar variability. A gain in elevation of approximately 1,000 feet can result in monthly total rainfall increases of 25 percent or more, and an equivalent decline in precipitation can be seen by moving 1,000 feet downward.

Flora and Fauna

The high desert of Bears Ears has a rich biological heritage, with a wide array of plants and animals adapted to the harsh environment.

The defining biome of the region is the pygmy forest, found in dry, rocky areas at elevations between 3,500 and 8,000 feet. Two types of trees characterize this forest, the Utah juniper and the pinyon pine. The small stature of these trees provides the name "pygmy"; the juniper grows to about 15 feet at maturity and the pinyon to about 35 feet. The trees' lack of height can be deceptive; what looks at first like a collection of bushes can actually be an old-growth forest, aged 500 years or more.

Both the pinyon and juniper are exceptionally slow-growing, constrained by the lack of moisture and nutrient-poor soil of their environment. However, what they lack in speed they make up for in persistence, surviving through extended periods of drought, freezing weather, and other hardships.

The top of Cedar Mesa is an excellent example of a juniper and pinyon wooded area. The name "Cedar Mesa" comes from the juniper, which was misidentified as a cedar by some early European settlers and is still occasionally labeled that way.

Other common plants seen in the pygmy forest include the yucca, prickly pear cactus, salt brush, and Mormon tea in flat areas and mountain mahogany, gambel oak, rabbitbrush, and serviceberry on slopes and hillsides.

Many birds nest or feed among the trees, most notably the pinyon jay and common raven, featured in multiple local Native American mythologies. Mule deer browse on the leaves and branches, and the

Claret cup cactus flowers.

Mule deer near Mule Canyon.

cottontail rabbit, black-tailed jackrabbit, pinyon mouse, least chipmunk, and rock squirrel lead a host of small mammals and rodents that inhabit the ground.

At elevations above 8,000 feet, heavier precipitation and lower temperatures lead to plant communities more typical of regions far to the north. Conifer forests predominate on Elk Ridge and around the Bears Ears Buttes, with stately ponderosa pines reaching to the sky. Rare stands of Douglas fir hang on to life in a few sheltered corners, showing remarkable hardiness for a tree that is most associated with the rain forests of the Pacific Northwest more than a thousand miles away.

High alpine slopes, especially in the Abajo Mountains, are often blanketed with quaking aspen, bringing the mountainsides alive with golden color in the fall. Elk, black bears, mule deer, and the occasional mountain lion roam the same territory.

At lower elevations, warmer and drier conditions prevail. Bordering Bears Ears to the northeast is what many archaeologists and biologists refer to as the Great Sage Plain, a large expanse of fertile flatlands. Western sagebrush dominates the landscape, with its distinctive aroma that for many people evokes the open land of much of the western United States.

On the floor of many canyons, conditions similar to those on the Great Sage Plain prevail and islands of sagebrush appear. Wherever the sage grows highest, up to 7 feet, the best quality soil can generally be found. These locations, typically earthen benches alongside creeks and streams, were used by the Ancestral Puebloans for planting their beans, squash, and corn.

Other plants cluster along the washes at the canyon bottoms, living on the collected runoff and groundwater. Thickets of willow often stabilize sandy banks, and thirsty cottonwood trees reach deep into the ground to find the moisture they need. Easily identified by their gnarled bark and sheer size, cottonwoods are generally the tallest trees by far anywhere in the canyons, providing welcome shade in the heat of the day. Just like their cousins the aspens, with whom they share spade-shaped leaves, cottonwoods turn golden yellow in the fall.

Animals that frequent the canyons include the lesser mammals from the pygmy forest and a host of small reptiles and amphibians, including the side-blotched lizard, northern sagebrush lizard, northern plateau lizard, Great Basin gopher snake, and red-spotted toad.

The prevalence of bighorn sheep as a motif in Ancestral Puebloan rock art indicates both the importance of this large ungulate to that culture and its relative abundance across the landscape. Unfortunately, bighorns are now rare, although recent efforts to reintroduce them to the area have shown some promise.

Geology

Although it's hard to imagine in the desert, millions of years ago southern Utah was the edge of a shallow sea. Over countless eons the water advanced and retreated, depositing endless layers of silt, mud, and sand. Time and pressure eventually hardened the layers into sedimentary rock, the signature red and yellow sandstones that now define the region.

The underlying land eventually began to rise, climbing thousands of feet into the air to create the Colorado Plateau. As the land rose, the forces of erosion from wind and water carved out the canyons, buttes, mesas, and hoodoos we see today. Some rocks still display their marine roots; in places where the sandstone forms bulbous domes, the slickrock is nothing more than ancient sand dunes, frozen in place.

One of the great pleasures of exploring the Colorado Plateau is seeing the infinite variety of rock formations on display. Arches, needles, towers,

Rainbows over Comb Ridge. JOSH EWING

MAJOR STRATA OF BEARS EARS AND CEDAR MESA

Name	Description	Max. Thickness	Landscape Feature	Geologic Period	Geologic Era
Navajo Sandstone	White or light brown sandstone displaying high-angle cross beds	~1,000 ft.	Top layer of Comb Ridge	Jurassic, 200 to 145 million years ago (mya)	Mesozoic, 250 to 65 mya
Kayenta Formation	Reddish-brown, thick-bedded sandstone	~350 ft.	Secondary layer of Comb Ridge, just above steep cliffs		
Wingate Sandstone	Pale red or deep red cross-bedded sandstone, forming steep walls and vertical cliffs	~375 ft.	Bears Ears Buttes; prominent red cliffs on west side of Comb Ridge		
Chinle Formation	Reddish, slope-forming sandstone mixed with layers of various other inclusions and colors	~650 ft.	Rubbly slopes at base of west side of Comb Ridge	Triassic, 250 to 200 mya	
Moenkopi Formation	Chocolate-brown and reddish-brown sandstone and siltstones	~1,000 ft.	Bottom of Comb Ridge		
Organ Rock Formation	Red and reddish-brown slates and siltstones	~300 ft.	Gentle slopes around mesas above Natural Bridges National Monument; floor of Comb Wash	Permian, 300 to 250 mya	Paleozoic, 540 to 250 mya
Cedar Mesa Sandstone	Light-colored and fine-grained quartz sandstone containing red layers of siltstone; frequently erodes into cliffs with alcoves	~1,200 ft.	Bridges at Natural Bridges National Monument; cliffs and alcoves of Cedar Mesa Canyons, especially Grand Gulch		
Elephant Canyon/Halgaito Shale Formations	Reddish, loose sandstones and siltstones and gray, hard limestones and shales	~800 ft.	Slopes below buttes and floor of Valley of the Gods		
Honaker Trail Formation	A mix of brownish and gray limestone and shale layers, often rich in ancient marine fossils	~3,000 ft.	Top part of the San Juan River gorge, with steeply sloped, crumbly walls	Pennsylvanian, 325 to 300 mya	
Paradox Formation	Hard gray and brown limestone layers	~5,000 ft.	Bottom part of the San Juan River gorge, with sheer cliff bands		

and countless other shapes that defy simple description are not just features of the landscape, they *are* the landscape.

National parks across the plateau, like Capitol Reef, Zion, Bryce, and Arches, are all world famous for their geology, showing the great variety of rocks available. The immense depth of the Grand Canyon takes this to an extreme, with its multicolored layers stacked thousands of feet down, the bones of the earth laid bare.

The same strata featured at the parks also run through the Bears Ears region, and are just as impressive in their shapes, sizes, and colors. It would take a lifetime to learn their entire history, and absolute mastery is beyond even some professional geologists. But it doesn't take a geologist or rock hound to appreciate the view, and a basic familiarity with what you are looking at only adds to the experience.

The chart on page 10 provides a quick reference to the major strata of Bear Ears and Cedar Mesa. As with everywhere else, younger rocks lie on top of older ones, and the deeper you go, the older they get. Note that not all layers are visible in all areas, and most of the time layers may be much thinner than the maximum thicknesses given in the table.

Also note that due to the folding and bending of strata across the landscape, particular layers may appear at markedly different elevations in different places. This is how the Wingate Sandstone can comprise both the Bears Ears Buttes at 8,500 feet and the red cliffs on the west side of Comb Ridge at 5,000 feet.

Archaeological History

No matter where you go in Bears Ears, you are walking in the footsteps of others who have come before. For thousands of years, people have traveled its canyons, mesas, and highlands, their lives intimately tied to the landscape. The rich cultural and archaeological history of Bears Ears is the legacy they left behind, a treasure chest of discovery for anyone who encounters it.

The earliest human traces in the region date back to the Archaic period (approximately 6500 BCE), when nomadic hunters first roamed the landscape. From this origin, the Basketmaker and then Pueblo societies grew and evolved over the centuries until the eventual abandonment of the Four Corners region around 1300 CE. These societies, whose people are now referred to as the Ancestral Puebloans, moved south and east to build Pueblos that are still in use today, at places like Hopi, Zuni, Taos, and Acoma.

CHRONOLOGY: GREATER FOUR CORNERS AREA

Dates	Periods	Distinctive Characteristics
1350–1600 CE	Pueblo IV	Large plaza-oriented pueblos in Rio Grande and western Pueblo areas; low kiva-to-room ratio; kachina cult widespread; corrugated pottery replaced by plain utility types; B/W pottery declines relative to red, orange, or yellow types.
1150–1350 CE	Pueblo III	Large pueblos and/or "revisionist great houses" in some areas, dispersed pattern in others; high kiva-to-room ratios; cliff dwellings; towers; triwalls; corrugated gray and elaborate B/W pottery, plus red or orange pottery in some areas; abandonment of the Four Corners by 1300.
900–1150 CE	Pueblo II	Chacoan florescence; "great houses," great kivas, roads, etc. in many but not all regions; strong differences between great houses and surrounding "unit pueblos," composed of a kiva and small surface masonry roomblock; corrugated gray and elaborate B/W pottery, plus decorated red or orange types in some areas.
750–900 CE	Pueblo I	Large villages in some areas; unit pueblos of "proto-kiva" plus surface roomblock of jacal or crude masonry; great kivas; plain and neckbanded gray pottery with low frequencies of B/W and decorated red ware.
500–750 CE	Basketmaker III	Habitation is deep pithouse plus surface storage pits, cists, or rooms; dispersed settlement with occasional small villages and occasional great kivas; plain gray pottery, small occurrences of B/W pottery; bow and arrow replaces atlatl; beans added to cultigens.
50–500 CE	Basketmaker II (late)	Habitation is shallow pithouse plus storage pits or cists; dispersed settlement with small, low-density villages in some areas; campsites important as well (?); no pottery; atlatl and dart; corn and squash but no beans; upland dry farming in addition to floodplain farming.
1500 BCE–50 CE	Basketmaker II (early)	Long-term seasonal (?) use of caves for camping, storage, burial, rock art; San Juan Anthropomorphic-style pictographs and petroglyphs; camp and limited activity sites in open; no pottery; atlatl and dart; corn and squash but no beans; cultivation primarily floodplain or runoff based (?).
6500–1500 BCE	Archaic	Subsistence based on wild foods; high mobility; low population density; shelters and open sites; atlatl and dart; no pottery.

CREDIT: © 1990 Crow Canyon Archaeological Center (Dr. William D. Lipe)

After the abandonment, other Native American groups such as the Navajos and Utes began to visit. They were followed by early Spanish explorers and later the first European settlers, all adding their own chapters to the story written on the land.

But it is the imprint left by the Ancestral Puebloans that is the most evocative for visitors today, with their ancient imagery drawn on the rocks, their pottery and arrowheads scattered on the ground, their houses, granaries, and kivas tucked into the cliffs. The first time you encounter an Ancestral Puebloan site in the bend of a canyon or on a sandstone precipice is an experience you will never forget.

It is nice to add some context to the sense of wonder you experience at these unique cultural sites. The table below provides descriptions of the key stages of Ancestral Puebloan society and their associated vestiges to help you identify them in the field. Note that in some places, structures, rock art, and artifacts are all found together, implying a direct linkage, but they may have been created centuries apart. Discerning these kinds of differences can be difficult for the amateur, but hopefully the table on page 12 will be a useful guide to the interpretation and understanding of any archaeological discoveries you might make.

Visit with Respect

Most hikers are already familiar with **Leave No Trace** principles, a set of basic guidelines to help minimize human impact on the landscape. Those principles can generally be boiled down to this: Leave an area just like you found it—if not better.

Following the ethic of leaving places just as you found them will serve you, and the landscape, well. But the cultural, archaeological, and natural treasures of Bears Ears also require additional care and attention for preservation.

The **Visit with Respect** program helps reduce impacts on the sensitive cultural landscape of Bears Ears by teaching visitors how to visit in a way that will preserve cultural sites unimpaired. This ensures that the history of those who came before remains intact, that other visitors can experience a sense of wonder, that archaeologists can learn about the past, and, more important, that current and future generations connected with this landscape can continue to visit these important sites.

The icons shown on pages 14 to 16 display the essence of visiting with respect. Throughout the text of this book, you will see some of these icons displayed as helpful reminders, like "Steer Clear of Walls" alongside a description of a fragile ruin.

Of course, every icon applies wherever you go, whether there is a particular icon shown in the text or not. Follow all the **Visit with Respect** guidelines and this remarkable landscape will remain unchanged long into the future. There is no experience quite like reaching a pristine cultural site in the wilderness and feeling as though you're the first person to see it in a thousand years. If you visit with respect, others who come behind you can have the same experience.

 LEAVE ALL ARTIFACTS: Keep discovery alive so the next person can share the experience. Every artifact contains a story. It's illegal to remove or take any artifact, including historic trash, from public lands.

 DON'T TOUCH ROCK IMAGERY OR MAKE YOUR OWN: Vandalism of petroglyphs and pictographs erases stories of ancient people and destroys the experience for future visitors.

 STEER CLEAR OF WALLS: Structures are easily damaged. Please refrain from touching, leaning, standing, or climbing on any structures.

 GUIDE CHILDREN THROUGH SITES: Archaeological sites are not playgrounds. Teach children to respect these places. Keep a close eye so they don't get hurt or accidentally damage cultural and natural resources.

 DOGS & ARCHAEOLOGY DON'T MIX: To prevent digging and erosion, pets are not allowed in archaeological sites. Please make sure pets are leashed and kept away from the site. Know beforehand where dogs are permitted.

 CAMP & EAT AWAY FROM ARCHAEOLOGY: Camping, fires, and food can damage the archaeological remains and also spoil the view for other visitors. Remember to pack out all waste.

DON'T BUILD CAIRNS: This form of ephemeral vandalism increases impacts on sensitive sites. Cairns are sometimes mistakenly constructed with artifacts. They also may mislead or disorient other visitors.

 DON'T DISTURB FOSSILS OR BONES: Leave fossils, dinosaur bones, tracks, and other paleontological remains where you find them so future visitors and scientists can learn from them.

 DON'T BUST THE CRUST: Stay on existing trails and routes to protect the living cryptobiotic soil. Once stepped on, this fragile crust takes years to regrow.

 USE RUBBER-TIPPED HIKING POLES: A rubber tip prevents your hiking pole from scratching and scarring rock images on the ground surface.

 PAY YOUR FEES: It may not seem like much, but your small fee helps support important monitoring, enforcement, and amenities like toilets.

 DON'T BUILD FIRE RINGS: Remember to check when and where fires are allowed. Where fires are allowed, use existing fire rings or bring your own fire pan.

 ENJOY ARCHAEOLOGY WITHOUT ROPES: The use of climbing gear like ropes to access archaeological sites is illegal. This protects archaeology from damage caused by falling rocks and looting.

 GPS REVEALS TOO MUCH: GPS points often lead uneducated visitors to sensitive sites. When posting online about your trip, remove all references to location.

 LEAVE GRINDING IN THE PAST: Regrinding in slicks and grooves removes the finish left by those who created them. Please refrain from touching or using grinding slicks.

STAY ON DESIGNATED ROADS: Use existing roads when traveling to cultural sites. Driving off road can create new routes on top of fragile archaeology and ecosystems.

 HISTORIC ARTIFACTS AREN'T TRASH: Leave historic artifacts like rusted cans where they are. They help interpret the past and show who has been here before.

 PACK OUT YOUR POOP: Human and pet waste threatens fragile desert ecosystems and drinking water sources for hikers and wildlife. Poop near cultural sites is disrespectful to indigenous cultures that hold this landscape sacred. When hiking and camping, please use portable waste bags or a camp toilet. When you just can't pack it out, do your best by burying your waste 6 inches deep.

Wilderness Restrictions, Regulations, and Permits

The Bears Ears region is a jumble of public lands, a tapestry of overlapping management groups, agencies, and interests.

Most of Bears Ears is currently run by the Bureau of Land Management (BLM), the federal agency tasked with handling the majority of public lands throughout the western United States. Within its aegis, various sections have received special designation, including Wilderness Study Areas and Instant Study Areas. These allotments could become congressionally mandated full wilderness areas sometime in the future. Canyon Rims Recreation Area and the Dark Canyon and Grand Gulch Primitive Areas are also overseen by the BLM.

Other federal and state agencies such as Utah State Parks, the US Forest Service, and the National Park Service manage additional pieces. These include Glen Canyon National Recreation Area, Natural Bridges National Monument, Goosenecks State Park, and Manti-La Sal National Forest.

This hodgepodge was already in place before the national monument was created in 2016 and then drastically reduced a year later, adding another layer of complexity. The legal status of the monument remains unresolved as of early 2021, and may yet be bubbling through the federal court system for many years. This leaves a great deal of uncertainty in what was already a complex land-management patchwork. With the system in so much flux, figuring out when, where, and for what activities land-use permits are needed can be a challenge.

To help clarify the situation, each destination chapter in this book indicates whether **Fees and Permits** are required. Note that this information was accurate when the book went to press, but *it is subject to change at any time.* The best resource for up-to-date information is the managing agency listed under **Contacts** for that particular trip.

Cedar Mesa and Moon House Permits

The bulk of trips requiring permits are on Cedar Mesa and nearby Butler Wash, all administered by the BLM's Monticello Field Office:

BLM Monticello Field Office
365 N. Main
PO Box 7
Monticello, UT 84535
(435) 587-1500
www.blm.gov/office/monticello-field-office

Monticello works in conjunction with the Kane Gulch Ranger Station (KGRS) on Cedar Mesa, the BLM's de facto visitor center:

Kane Gulch Ranger Station
UT 261, 4 miles south of UT 95
(no public phone)

Cedar Mesa Day-Use Permits

Day-use hiking permits are required for entry into all Cedar Mesa canyons (except Johns Canyon) and their tributaries: Grand Gulch, Fish and Owl Canyons, Slickhorn Canyon, Road Canyon, Lime Creek Canyon, and Mule Canyon (including the North and South Forks). McLoyd Canyon, home to Moon House Ruin, requires a special permit (see below).

Day-use permits are also required for entry into sites along Butler Wash Road and Comb Ridge.

No reservations are required for day-use permits, but there is a fee and groups are restricted to a maximum of twelve people. The permits can be acquired at self-pay kiosks at the trailheads and on the mesa top year-round, or at KGRS when it is open during the spring and fall seasons (9 a.m.–noon daily, March 1–June 15 and September 1–October 31).

An annual vehicle pass is also available, but it can only be acquired at KGRS.

Moon House Day-Use Permits

A special day-use permit is required year-round to visit Moon House Ruin in McLoyd Canyon. Reservations are generally required and permits are issued on a first-come, first-served basis. A maximum of twenty visitors are allowed per day and the maximum group size is twelve people.

During the spring and fall high seasons (March 1–June 15 and September 1–October 31), twelve of the twenty available spaces each day can be reserved ahead of time and the remaining eight spaces are available on a walk-in basis at KGRS between 9 a.m. and noon the day of the trip. Reservations can be made online at least five days but no more than ninety days ahead of the entry date. All permits must be picked up in person at KGRS the morning of the hike.

During the summer and winter low seasons (June 16–August 31 and November 1–February 28), Moon House day-use permits must be reserved at least five days but no more than ninety days ahead of the entry date. Since KGRS is closed, there are no walk-in permits available at this time. For reservations within five days of the entry date, call the permit desk at the BLM Monticello Field Office at (435) 587-1510.

Moon House permits require a fee and can be reserved online at recreation.gov/permits/273374.

Cedar Mesa Backpacking Permits

Backpacking permits are required to camp overnight for one or more nights in any of the Cedar Mesa canyons that require day-use permits (see page 17). No camping is allowed in McLoyd Canyon (Moon House Ruin).

During the spring and fall high seasons (March 1–June 15 and September 1–October 31), twenty visitors each day are allowed to enter the canyons from each Cedar Mesa trailhead. Of the twenty available spaces, twelve can be reserved at least five days but no more than ninety days ahead of time, and the remaining eight are available on a walk-in basis at KGRS between 9 a.m. and noon the first day of the trip. All permits must be picked up in person at KGRS the morning the hike begins. The maximum group size is twelve people.

During the summer and winter low seasons (June 16–August 31 and November 1–February 28), backpacking permits can be acquired at self-pay kiosks at trailheads and on the mesa top. No reservations are needed.

Backpacking permits require a fee and can be reserved online for trips during the high season at recreation.gov/permits/273374.

Note that car camping on the mesa top does not currently require a permit.

More information on the Cedar Mesa permit system is available online at www.blm.gov/programs/recreation/permits-and-passes/lotteries-and-permit-systems/utah/cedarmesa.

Visitor Resources

There is currently no unified visitor center in Bears Ears to provide interpretive displays, maps, permits, information, and all other items needed by tourists. Instead, a number of different locations provide separate pieces to varying degrees. Each of the three locations listed below has something unique to offer, and a visit to any can prove worthwhile.

Bears Ears Education Center
567 W. Main St.
Bluff, UT 84512
(435) 414-0343
www.friendsofcedarmesa.org/bears-ears-center/
9am–5pm Thursday–Monday, March–November

Bears Ears Education Center in Bluff, Utah.

Visit with Respect information board.

Conceived, built, and maintained by advocacy group Friends of Cedar Mesa, the Bears Ears Education Center opened in the town of Bluff in fall of 2018. This unique venture is a grassroots-powered education center dedicated to helping visitors get the most out of a trip to the area without having a negative impact on irreplaceable cultural resources. Not a single penny of government funding went into the project, as it was developed by private donations from around the world, and a team of volunteers currently provides staffing and keeps it running day to day. Inside, local experts can answer any of your questions about where to go, what to see, and how to get there, with particular emphasis on encountering archaeo-logical and cultural sites with the Visit with Respect program. The center also features photographic exhibits, special speakers and events, and many other resources highlighting the attractions and wonders of the Bears Ears region.

Kane Gulch Ranger Station (KGRS)
UT 261, 4 miles south of UT 95
(no public phone)
9am–noon daily, March 1–June 15 and September 1–October 31

Kane Gulch Ranger Station.

Anyone who needs a Cedar Mesa day hiking or backpacking permit will come to KGRS to pick it up—but that's hardly the only reason to visit. Beyond issuing permits, the rangers at Kane Gulch have the best and most up-to-date information on everything needed for a trip into the backcountry: the availability of springs and water sources, local road access, expected weather, trail conditions, and much more. KGRS is the public face of the BLM for the entire Bears Ears region, but the rangers'

Ancestral Puebloan art and culture educational display.

knowledge extends beyond just the lands managed by the BLM; they can generally answer questions and provide assistance for areas handled by other management agencies as well. On top of that, the "Cedar Mesa Through Time: Place, Archaeology, and Culture" exhibit featured inside the station rivals anything found in a museum, and is alone worth the time to visit.

Edge of the Cedars State Park Museum
660 W. 400 N.
Blanding, UT 84511
(435) 678-2238
https://stateparks.utah.gov/parks/edge-of-the-cedars/
9am–5pm Monday–Saturday, 9am–4pm Sunday
(hours may vary seasonally; some holiday closures)

The Edge of the Cedars State Park Museum has one of the greatest collections of Ancestral Puebloan artifacts available anywhere. Its regularly rotating exhibits showcase such remarkable items as a sash made out of

Edge of the Cedars Pueblo.

Ancestral Puebloan pottery.

Artifacts at Edge of the Cedars State Park Museum.

scarlet macaw feathers and the original wooden ladder from the Perfect Kiva Ruin (see Trip 19). The unrivaled pottery collection consists of hundreds of separate pieces and artistic styles from across the Four Corners region, most of them complete and intact. Local artists are often featured in the galleries, and, in a particularly nice touch, items discovered in the backcountry by amateurs are prominently displayed alongside their finders' stories. Outside, the main building stands next to the remnants of an actual Ancestral Puebloan structure, complete with an accessible kiva.

How to Use This Guide

Each region begins with a **section introduction**, where you're given a sweeping look at the lay of the land. After this general overview, chapters are presented that feature specific hiking or driving destinations within that region.

To aid in quick decision-making, each chapter begins with an overview. These short summaries give you a taste of the specific adventure to follow. Next, you'll find the quick, nitty-gritty details of the trip: where the start is located, trip length, approximate time required, difficulty rating, best season, trip contacts (for updates on conditions), and more. The **Finding the trailhead** or **Finding the start** section gives you dependable directions from the nearest town right down to where the trip begins, including where to park your car for a hike. The **description** is the meat of the chapter. Detailed and honest, it's the author's carefully researched impression of the destination. While it's impossible to cover everything, you can rest assured that we won't miss what's important. In **Miles and Directions**, we provide mileage cues to identify all significant landmarks, route directions, and points of interest. Some destinations also provide additional information at the end on special precautions, nearby camping opportunities, or other related attractions.

Overview

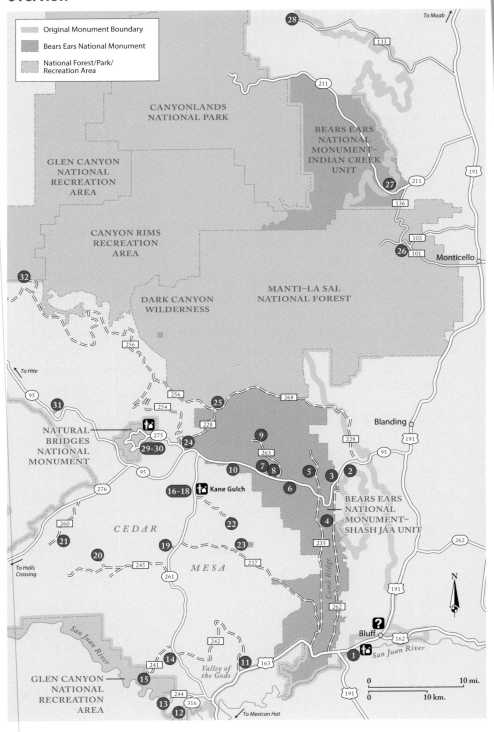

Legend:
- Original Monument Boundary
- Bears Ears National Monument
- National Forest/Park/Recreation Area

To Moab

CANYONLANDS NATIONAL PARK

BEARS EARS NATIONAL MONUMENT–INDIAN CREEK UNIT

GLEN CANYON NATIONAL RECREATION AREA

CANYON RIMS RECREATION AREA

MANTI–LA SAL NATIONAL FOREST

DARK CANYON WILDERNESS

Monticello

To Hite

Blanding

NATURAL BRIDGES NATIONAL MONUMENT

Kane Gulch

BEARS EARS NATIONAL MONUMENT–SHASH JÁA UNIT

CEDAR MESA

Comb Ridge

To Halls Crossing

San Juan River

Valley of the Gods

Bluff

San Juan River

GLEN CANYON NATIONAL RECREATION AREA

To Mexican Hat

N

0   10 mi.
0   10 km.

Trip Finder

Best Trips for Ruins
  3. Butler Wash Ruins (Hike)
  4. Fishmouth Cave (Hike)
  5. Arch Canyon Ruin and Trail (Hike)
  6. Cave Towers Ruin (Hike)
  7. Mule Canyon Kiva (Drivable Landmark)
  8. House on Fire Ruin (Hike)
 16. Junction Ruin (Hike)
 17. Turkey Pen Ruin (Hike)
 18. Split Level Ruin (Backpack)
 19. Perfect Kiva Ruin (Hike)
 21. Banister Ruin (Hike)
 23. Moon House Ruin (Hike)

Best Trips for Rock Art
  1. Sand Island Petroglyph Panel (Drivable Landmark)
 20. Big Man Pictograph Panel (Hike)
 27. Newspaper Rock Petroglyph Panel (Drivable Landmark)
 30. Natural Bridges Loop Hike (Hike)

Best Trips for Viewpoints
  9. Arch Canyon Overlook #1 (Drivable Landmark)
 10. Salvation Knoll (Hike)
 12. Goosenecks State Park (Drivable Landmark)
 14. Moki Dugway (Scenic Drive)
 15. Muley Point Lookout (Drivable Landmark)
 24. Bears Ears Buttes (Drivable Landmark)
 25. Arch Canyon Overlook #2 (Drivable Landmark)
 28. Needles Overlook (Drivable Landmark)

Best Trips for Geology/Rock Formations
  3. Butler Wash Ruins (Hike)
  4. Fishmouth Cave (Hike)
  9. Arch Canyon Overlook #1 (Drivable Landmark).

The San Juan River winds through the southern Bears Ears region. JOSH EWING

Best Easy Trips/Trips for Children
1. Sand Island Petroglyph Panel (Drivable Landmark)
2. Butler Wash Dinosaur Tracks (Hike)
3. Butler Wash Ruins (Hike)
6. Cave Towers Ruin (Hike)
7. Mule Canyon Kiva (Drivable Landmark)
8. House on Fire Ruin (Hike)
10. Salvation Knoll (Hike)
11. Valley of the Gods (Scenic Drive)
12. Goosenecks State Park (Drivable Landmark)
14. Moki Dugway (Scenic Drive)
26. Harts Draw Road (Scenic Drive)
28. Needles Overlook (Drivable Landmark)
29. Natural Bridges Loop Drive (Scenic Drive)
31. Fry Canyon Ruin (Drivable Landmark)

Best Trips for Physical Challenge
4. Fishmouth Cave (Hike)
16. Junction Ruin (Hike)
17. Turkey Pen Ruin (Hike)
18. Split Level Ruin (Backpack)
19. Perfect Kiva Ruin (Hike)
20. Big Man Pictograph Panel (Hike)
21. Banister Ruin (Hike)
22. Fish and Owl Canyons (Backpack)
23. Moon House Ruin (Hike)
30. Natural Bridges Loop Hike (Hike)
32. Sundance Trail (Hike)

Map Legend

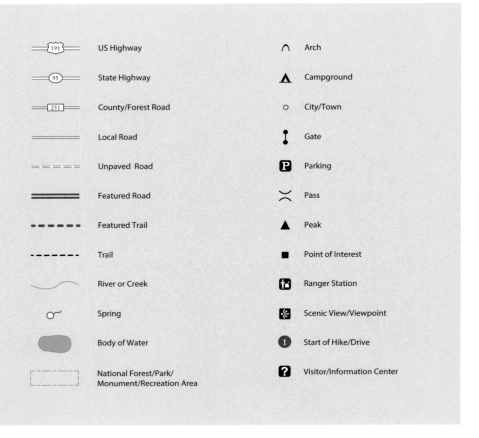

US Highway

State Highway

County/Forest Road

Local Road

Unpaved Road

Featured Road

Featured Trail

Trail

River or Creek

Spring

Body of Water

National Forest/Park/
Monument/Recreation Area

Arch

Campground

City/Town

Gate

Parking

Pass

Peak

Point of Interest

Ranger Station

Scenic View/Viewpoint

Start of Hike/Drive

Visitor/Information Center

Comb Ridge/Butler Wash Region

THE GREAT SANDSTONE FIN OF COMB RIDGE STRETCHES MORE THAN 75 miles from the town of Kayenta, Arizona, to where it fades into the Abajo (Blue) Mountains in Utah at its northern end. Both a significant landmark for navigation and a substantial barrier to east–west travel, the Comb is one of the most recognizable topographical features anywhere in Bears Ears. The trips in this section explore the rich archaeological heritage of the Comb's many fissures, gaps, and clefts, as well as visit Butler Wash, the Comb's major drainage channel to the east, which holds some treasures of its own.

Ruin alcove near Fishmouth Cave.

1 Sand Island Petroglyph Panel (Drivable Landmark)

An excellent rock art panel easily accessible just outside the town of Bluff.

Don't Touch Rock Imagery or Make Your Own

Visiting time: Up to 1 hour
Best season: Year-round
Canine compatibility: Leashed dogs allowed
Fees and permits: None
MAPS: USGS topo maps: Bluff, Utah; **Other maps:** National Geographic Trails Illustrated #706, Grand Gulch Cedar Mesa Plateau
Contacts: BLM Monticello Field Office, 365 N. Main, PO Box 7, Monticello, UT 84535, (435) 587-1500, www.blm.gov/office/monticello-field-office; **Other:** Sand Island Ranger Station, "A Loop" Road, Sand Island Campground
Finding the trailhead: From the town of Bluff, take Main Street/US 191 south for about 3 miles and turn left at the signed entrance to Sand Island Boat Launch and Campground. Enter the campground and then take the first right onto a gravel road, signed for "Sand Island Petroglyph Panel." In about 0.3 mile, park at the information board on the right.
GPS coordinates: N37° 15.71160' / W109° 37.11420'

The Panel

For centuries people have accessed the San Juan River at Sand Island, currently home to a campground and boat launch. The car campers and river runners of today are walking in the footsteps of the Ancestral Puebloans, who marked the site with an extensive art panel, still visible on the rock. Some of the symbols displayed date back at least 3,000 years.

Look for the art along the sandstone wall directly behind the information board. Note that a fence runs along the base of the wall to keep viewers from touching or otherwise harming the display; please respect it. Regrettably, vandals have already applied modern graffiti in several spots.

The petroglyphs start far up to the right, above a sloping sandstone ledge where the artists likely stood while they worked. But on the left, you will notice much of the art is now mysteriously out of reach. The ancient

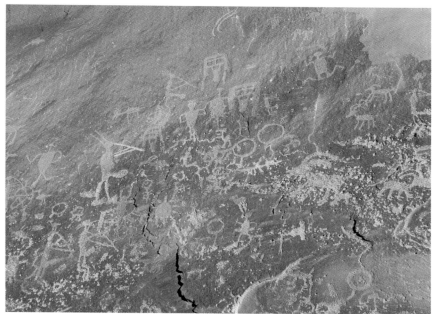

Ancient petroglyphs at Sand Island.

Puebloans must have climbed up somehow, although it's hard to imagine with this approach how they would have had a free hand left for drawing, or even been able to effectively see their work.

The entire panel exhibits a mix of concrete and abstract forms. Life-size handprints, bighorn sheep, and hunters with weapons sit next to spirals, dotted lines, and geometric patterns. Images are frequently crowded together or even overlapping, a layering known as superimposition.

These jumbled symbols and figures are hardly the work of a single artist, or even a single era. Some of the petroglyphs have been on the wall so long they have become revarnished. Others show evidence of repecking, a technique where later artists reemphasize the importance of an image long after its original creation.

The densest part of the panel features an artistic style common along the San Juan River known as San Juan Anthropomorphic. This style dates primarily from the early Basketmaker II period, roughly from 1500 BCE to 50 CE, when many archaeologists identify Ancestral Puebloan art as having reached its creative peak. "Anthropomorph" is a fancy word for "person"; one of the defining features of San Juan Anthropomorphic style

Sand Island Petroglyph Panel

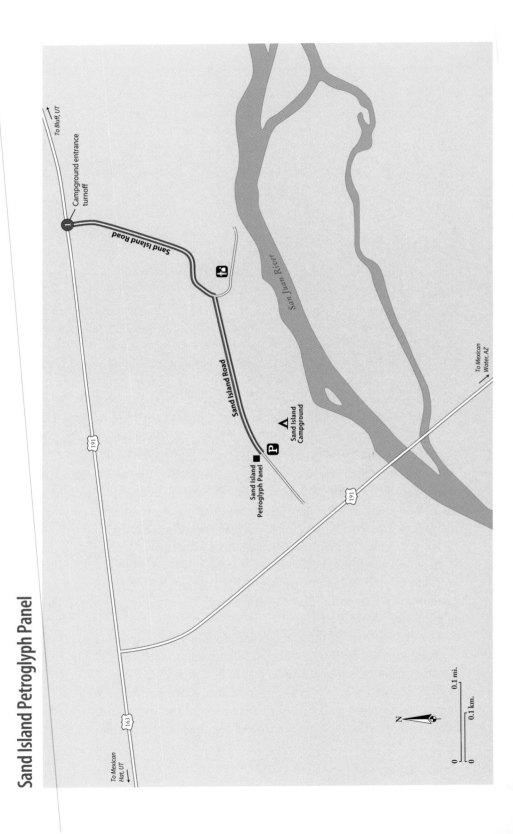

is its use of humanoid figures, generally broad-shouldered, facing the viewer, and sporting distinctive hairstyles or elaborate headgear.

Look for multiple images of the trickster Kokopelli above the center of the gallery. This shamanistic figure represents music and fertility and is traditionally shown in a hunchbacked stance with a long flute and a feathered headdress. The Kokopellis here, however, are conspicuously straight-backed.

Kokopelli might look familiar; he has become ubiquitous in the modern era. Representing both the southwestern United States and New Age free-spiritedness, he appears in stylized form to sell everything from herbal teas to mountain bikes.

It's easy to relate to an image of Kokopelli when you've seen him plastered on your coffee mug in the town of Bluff that morning. The same is true for the timeless drama of a man hunting a bighorn sheep. But spirals, wavy lines, or connected boxes do not have obvious interpretations for the modern viewer.

Whatever meaning you draw from the art is not likely to match what the original artists intended—or even what others around you might think. The experience of viewing the petroglyphs at Sand Island will be unique to each individual.

After following the length of the fence to view the panel in detail, it is worth returning to your car via the road. This broader vantage allows you to view the entire wall all at once, giving a sense of both the vastness of the sandstone canvas and the range of the petroglyphs on display.

Special attractions: The boat launch provides access to the San Juan River for river runners. Permits are required and typically must be reserved months in advance through a lottery system. Anyone is welcome to watch the activity at the launch as teams prepare to set out on the water.

Vehicle campsites: Camping is available at Sand Island Campground. The campground is open year-round, and reservations are not generally required unless you have a large group. Fees are payable via drop box envelope.

2 Butler Wash Dinosaur Tracks (Hike)

A short walk to some 160-million-year-old dinosaur footprints.

Don't Disturb Fossils or Bones

Start: Trailhead at the parking pullout
Distance: 0.2 mile out and back
Elevation gain: None
Hiking time: Up to 1 hour
Difficulty: Very easy (flat and extremely short)
Trail surface: Packed dirt and stone
Best season: Any time when dry
Canine compatibility: Dogs allowed
Fees and permits: None
MAPS: USGS topo maps: Black Mesa Butte, Utah; **Other maps:** National Geographic Trails Illustrated #706, Grand Gulch Cedar Mesa Plateau
Trail contacts: BLM Monticello Field Office, 365 N. Main, PO Box 7, Monticello, UT 84535, (435) 587-1500, www.blm.gov/office/monticello-field-office; **Other (seasonal):** Kane Gulch Ranger Station, UT 261, 4 miles south of UT 95
Finding the trailhead: From the town of Blanding, take US 191 south for about 3 miles and turn right onto UT 95. Follow UT 95 west for 9.4 miles and turn left just past milepost 112 onto San Juan CR (SJC) 262. Take the red-dirt SJC 262 over a cattle guard and then another 0.2 mile to a parking pullout on the right with an information sign. Note that you only have to go a short distance on SJC 262, but nonetheless it may be impassable when wet.
GPS coordinates: N37° 32.07180' / W109° 37.00560'

The Hike

So much of Bears Ears is dedicated to the ancients—at least what we call the ancients, the people who lived here in centuries past. The earliest known evidence of human activity in Bears Ears is no more than 10,000 years old, dating back to the hunter-gatherer societies of the Archaic period. But this hike can take you to something truly ancient, a set of dinosaur footprints left on a muddy ocean shoreline 160 million years ago.

Sizing up a theropod footprint.

Looking at the high desert around Butler Wash today, it's hard to picture a shallow sea lapping up against your feet. It's just as hard to grasp the vast amount of time that has passed since the Jurassic period, when the dinosaurs left their mark. The sandstone fin of Comb Ridge, one of the defining elements of the landscape, was thrust out of the ground about 65 million years ago. At that time, the dinosaur tracks had already existed for close to 100 million years.

Determining the age of dinosaur fossils is often mistaken as the work of archaeologists. But archaeology is properly the study of human history and prehistory; it is paleontologists who study dinosaurs—or, to be exact, the fossilized remains of dinosaurs. Bears Ears is renowned for its

Butler Wash Dinosaur Tracks

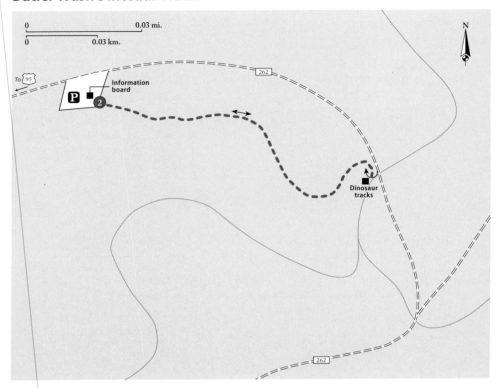

archaeology, but a visit to the Butler Wash Dinosaur Tracks gives you the chance to play amateur paleontologist.

Be sure to sign the trail register in the parking area and then review the information board for a primer on the three-toed theropods (meat-eaters) whose footprints you have come to see.

However, be aware that the information board is somewhat deceptive. The photos on the board were taken during optimal light conditions, with deep shadows making the footprints stand out. Most of the time you will not have this kind of light. Worse, the board says to watch for additional signage at the tracks themselves, but no such signs exist. Locating the tracks without these clues is by far the hardest thing about this hike.

The blink-and-you've-missed-it trail starts next to the information board and heads across the sagebrush plain. Before you've lost sight of your car you will reach the other end, where a few quick steps down the embankment bring you to the fossil site.

Just below the embankment an open stone slab tilts gently toward the wash from the dirt road on the left (east). The tracks are in this rock layer, three separate prints in a roughly linear alignment marching from east to west.

The tracks may be marked with cairns or stones to help you identify them. On the other hand, they also may be filled with sand or otherwise obscured. If you have trouble finding them, your best bet is to stand by the road, face the wash, and scan the stone surface at your feet for the shallow impressions.

It's easy to think that these dinosaur tracks must be impervious to harm; after all, they've been here for millions of years, withstanding geologic upheavals like the creation of Comb Ridge along the way. But they are actually quite fragile; the equivalent of thousands of years of erosion can be replicated with a few careless steps. Treat these dinosaur tracks with respect so others can enjoy them, maybe for another 100 million years.

Miles and Directions

0.0 Start from the trailhead.

0.1 Reach the dinosaur tracks site.

0.2 End back at the trailhead.

3 Butler Wash Ruins (Hike)

A compelling cluster of ruins in a dramatic setting on Comb Ridge.

Don't Bust the Crust

Start: Trailhead at the parking area
Distance: 1 mile out and back
Elevation gain: 100 feet
Hiking time: 1–2 hours
Difficulty: Easy due to short distance and minimal climb
Trail surface: Sandy dirt and rock, open slickrock
Best season: Year-round
Canine compatibility: Leashed dogs allowed
Fees and permits: None
MAPS: USGS topo maps: Hotel Rock, Utah; **Other maps:** National Geographic Trails Illustrated #706, Grand Gulch Cedar Mesa Plateau
Trail contacts: BLM Monticello Field Office, 365 N. Main, PO Box 7, Monticello, UT 84535, (435) 587-1500, www.blm.gov/office/monticello-field-office; **Other (seasonal):** Kane Gulch Ranger Station, UT 261, 4 miles south of UT 95
Finding the trailhead: From the town of Blanding, take US 191 south for about 3 miles and turn right onto UT 95. Follow UT 95 west for 10.5 miles and turn right just past a sign for "Butler Wash Indian Ruins." Follow the paved road as it climbs around to the right to reach the circular parking area.
GPS coordinates: N37° 31.46160' / W109° 37.94580'

The Hike

This easy trail offers one of the best ways to explore Comb Ridge and leads to an exemplary set of ruins. As a bonus, displays along the way showcase the flora of the high desert, highlighting signature local species like western sagebrush and narrow-leaf yucca.

The trail starts from the north end of the parking lot through a gap in the fence. The first section of the hike doubles as a nature trail, developed by local advocacy group Friends of Cedar Mesa. Interpretive signs detail the various types of plants that grow here along with lists of their

Butler Wash Ruins from the overlook.

traditional names and uses by local Native American tribes. There are also a few benches where you can rest and enjoy the view.

About two-thirds of the way along, the route exits the forest of junipers and pinyon pines to cross open slickrock. Obvious cairns mark the way, mortared and anchored into place. In a few sections stones have been laid on both sides of the route, like you might find along a garden path.

The trail ends at the fenced ruin overlook, complete with another bench and interpretive sign. Note the sheer number of alcoves, recesses, and overhanging ledges that are scattered all around the head of the canyon.

The largest alcoves stand to the right, toward the crest of Comb Ridge. You can see the dark line where water seeps through the various rock layers before reaching the sandy floor, 100 feet down. The biggest ruin stands in line with the water path, behind a collecting pool and a line of

Butler Wash Ruins

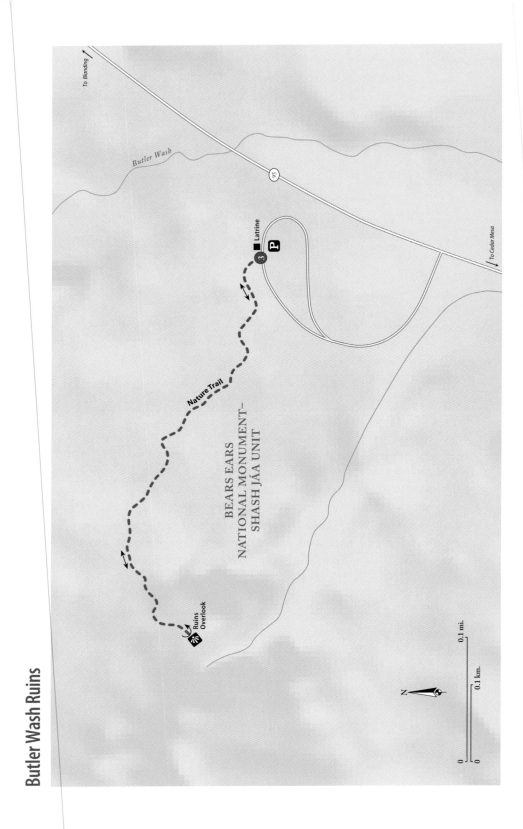

To Blanding

Butler Wash

95

To Cedar Mesa

Latrine

P

3

Nature Trail

BEARS EARS
NATIONAL MONUMENT–
SHASH JÁA UNIT

Ruins
Overlook

N

0   0.1 mi.
0   0.1 km.

brush. It is difficult to tell from the overlook, but this ruin contains four distinctive kivas.

Kivas were typically dug into the ground with only the roof reaching above the surface. However, constructing a kiva in an alcove like this required some adaptations since the bedrock prevented any kind of excavation. Instead, aboveground kivas had to be used, the common form in cliff dwellings.

The kivas here display two distinct designs. Three of the kivas are in the circular Mesa Verde style, but the fourth kiva, the one farthest to the right (north), is built in the square Kayenta style. This merging of styles in a single site is unusual and shows that the Butler Wash Ruins had cultural influences from both the east, where circular kivas predominated, and the south, where square ones prevailed.

Beyond the kivas, there are about twenty rooms in the main alcove and many smaller structures in the surrounding alcoves. Some of the outlying ruins are recessed so deeply that they are hard to make out unless the light is just right.

This site was likely in use starting around 500 CE, but most of the structures date from the Pueblo III period (1150–1350 CE). The sheer number of occupied alcoves along with the multiple types of available structures—including family dwellings, ceremonial kivas, and storage rooms—show that this canyon once housed a vibrant Ancestral Puebloan community.

As you view the site today, it's worth noting how inaccessible the ruins have become. What was once a thriving settlement was abandoned around 1300 CE, and whatever methods the residents used to get around these alcoves have long been lost to time.

Miles and Directions

0.0 Start from trailhead at parking area.

0.5 Reach Butler Wash Ruins overlook.

1.0 End back at the trailhead.

4 Fishmouth Cave (Hike)

An archaeology-rich hike that leads to a giant cave on Comb Ridge once used by the ancients.

Steer Clear of Walls

Start: Trailhead at the parking area
Distance: 2.8 miles out and back
Elevation gain: 500 feet
Hiking time: 2–4 hours
Difficulty: Easy to sandstone amphitheater; moderate to cave entrance, due to route-finding and tricky climbing
Trail surface: Sandy dirt and rock
Best season: Any time when dry
Canine compatibility: Leashed dogs allowed, but not in cave or other archaeological sites
Fees and permits: Cedar Mesa day-use permit required
MAPS: USGS topo maps: Bluff NW, Utah; **Other maps:** National Geographic Trails Illustrated #706, Grand Gulch Cedar Mesa Plateau
Trail contacts: BLM Monticello Field Office, 365 N. Main, PO Box 7, Monticello, UT 84535, (435) 587-1500, www.blm.gov/office/monticello-field-office; **Other (seasonal):** Kane Gulch Ranger Station, UT 261, 4 miles south of UT 95
Finding the trailhead: From the town of Blanding, take US 191 south for about 3 miles and turn right onto UT 95. Follow UT 95 west for 9.4 miles and turn left just past milepost 112 onto San Juan CR (SJC) 262. (Note that this road may be impassable when wet and that some maps may show it as San Juan CR 230.) Take the red-dirt SJC 262 for 0.3 mile and then stay right at a junction. Follow SJC 262 for another 8.2 miles, pass through a fence line, and then immediately turn right. Follow this doubletrack road for another 0.2 mile to the parking area.
GPS coordinates: N37° 25.66560' / W109° 37.96800'

The Hike

Fishmouth Cave stands high on the east face of Comb Ridge, visible from miles around. It's impossible not to wonder what's inside this yawning cavern, inviting exploration to anyone who sees it.

Approaching Fishmouth Cave.

To explore it for yourself, start walking from the parking lot at the end of the road to drop into Butler Wash. At the bottom of the slope, turn right where the road becomes a trail and then follow it up a draw to the west. Watch for the occasional brown vertical post with a hiking symbol to keep you on track.

Continue through a sagebrush meadow below a sandstone ledge on the right (north). After 0.4 mile, reach a Y-shaped confluence where two separate draws combine to form the one you have been following so far. Cross the nearer (northern) wash beneath some cottonwood trees and then head upcanyon in the southern one. The gaping mouth of your destination can be spotted through the branches overhead.

As you continue west, the sandstone walls close in and the draw becomes a more pronounced gully. At 0.6 mile, watch for a large alcove on the right, housing a fine collection of Ancestral Puebloan structures. A spur trail allows you to reach the alcove, but be sure to stay behind the chain as you admire the ancient buildings.

Inside Fishmouth Cave.

A little farther along, a second large alcove on the right shelters another set of ruins. This alcove and the one before it both face south, the typical orientation for habitation sites during the Pueblo II and Pueblo III eras. As you continue up the canyon, notice how similar alcoves on the left side are largely devoid of significant structures, although some contain rudimentary wall remnants. These north-facing alcoves were generally used during the earlier Basketmaker era, which had much more limited architecture.

At 0.9 mile another large, south-facing alcove stands noticeably empty of ruins. This alcove rests on the canyon floor and is thus unsuitable for permanent construction, owing to the risk of flooding from the wash.

Past this point the canyon narrows further and the trail climbs up into an open sandstone amphitheater. The entrance to Fishmouth Cave lies directly up the slope.

Some visitors may be content to enjoy the amphitheater as its own destination. If you continue up to the cave, expect the hike to become more challenging for the final ascent. Multiple social trails climb through the steep boulders and scree, requiring some route-finding through the loose and tricky footing.

Fishmouth Cave

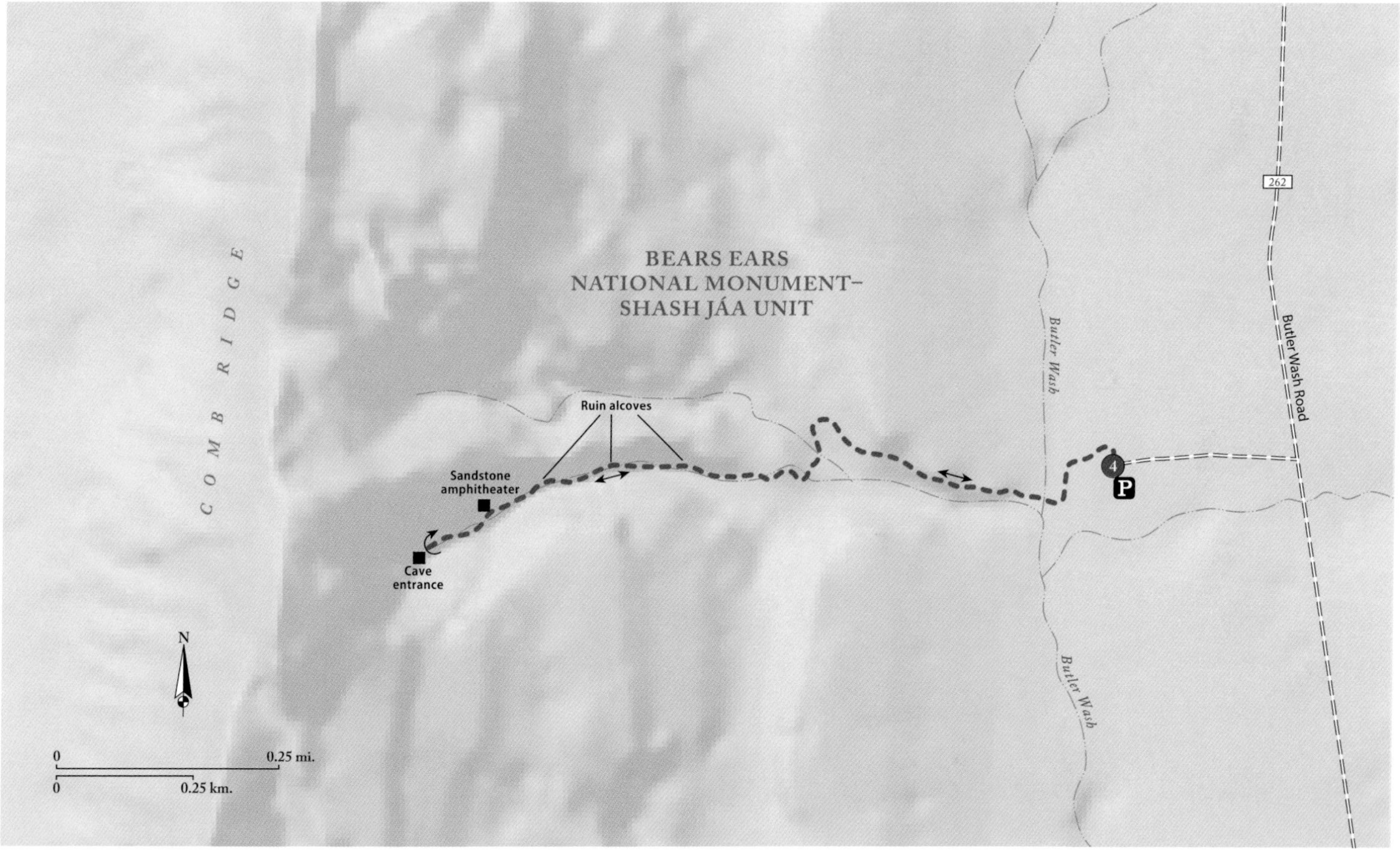

Butler Wash Road

262

Butler Wash

Butler Wash

P

4

BEARS EARS
NATIONAL MONUMENT–
SHASH JÁA UNIT

Ruin alcoves

Sandstone amphitheater

Cave entrance

COMB RIDGE

N

0   0.25 mi.

0   0.25 km.

At the top of the scramble, a step into the shade of Fishmouth Cave will offer sudden relief from the sun. After your eyes adjust, you can begin to appreciate the cave's vast size. Until you have stood under the domed ceiling and listened to your voice echo off the walls, it's difficult to really grasp the volume of this sandstone cathedral. A comparison with the typically sized alcoves you saw on the approach gives a sense of just how far beyond the norm Fishmouth Cave really is.

Follow the footpath upward through the dust to reach the rear wall. Unfortunately, acres of graffiti mar the back of the cave, much of it depressingly recent. But if you look carefully you can find some of the ancient rock art left here centuries earlier, including a prominent pictograph of three negative handprints.

Don't Touch Rock Imagery or Make Your Own

There are no major ruins here, but similarly to the north-facing alcoves you saw earlier, there are the remains of some Basketmaker shelters. There are also a few artifacts, including dried corncobs and the worn grooves for grinding called metates, scoured into the top of several boulders.

Leave Grinding in the Past

Gaze out from the cave entrance to enjoy the view from this high perch; you should be able to make out your car and the road you drove in on. Return the way you came.

Miles and Directions

0.0   Start from trailhead at parking area.

0.4   Cross the wash.

0.6–0.9   Pass multiple ruin alcoves on the right (north) wall.

1.1   Reach the sandstone amphitheater below the cave.

1.4   Reach the Fishmouth Cave entrance.

2.8   End back at the trailhead.

5 Arch Canyon Ruin and Trail (Hike)

An easy hike to a notable archaeological site with additional options to explore a giant canyon.

Steer Clear of Walls

Start: Arch Canyon Trailhead
Distance: 0.8 mile out and back to ruin; up to 24 miles or more out and back for the entire canyon
Elevation gain: Minimal to ruin; variable beyond
Hiking time: 1–2 hours for ruin; variable beyond
Difficulty: Easy to ruin; variable beyond
Trail surface: Dirt, rock, and deep sand
Best season: Spring and fall, when dry
Canine compatibility: Leashed dogs allowed
Fees and permits: Cedar Mesa day-use permit required
MAPS: USGS topo maps: Hotel Rock, Utah, for ruin and lower canyon; South Long Point and Kigalia Point, Utah, for upper canyon; **Other maps:** National Geographic Trails Illustrated #703, Manti-La Sal National Forest
Trail contacts: Lower canyon and ruin: BLM Monticello Field Office, 365 N. Main, PO Box 7, Monticello, UT 84535, (435) 587-1500, www.blm.gov/office/ monticello-field-office; **Other (seasonal):** Kane Gulch Ranger Station, UT 261, 4 miles south of UT 95; **Upper canyon:** Manti-La Sal National Forest, Main Office, 599 W. Price River Dr., Price, UT 84501, (435) 637-2817, www.fs .usda.gov/mantilasal; **Other:** Manti-La Sal National Forest, Monticello Office, 432 E. Center St., P.O. Box 820, Monticello, UT 84535, (435) 587-2041
Finding the trailhead: From the town of Blanding, take US 191 south for about 3 miles and turn right onto UT 95. Follow UT 95 west for 14.3 miles. Right after crossing Comb Wash, turn right onto San Juan CR 205. Go north on red-dirt SJC 205 for 2.3 miles to pass through a gate. Once through the gate stay right for another 0.1 mile until the road forks. Turn left to avoid crossing Arch Canyon Wash and go another 0.1 mile to pass through a fence and reach the parking area under a large cottonwood tree. Additional parking is available in another 0.1 mile, but the road surface may be rough and difficult to drive.
GPS coordinates: N37° 32.70900' / W109° 39.99600'

The Hike

The way into Arch Canyon is a rough, multiuse dirt road, and it's possible you will share the route with 4WD vehicles, mountain bikes, or even equestrians. But you can enjoy Arch Canyon on foot, especially if you just want to make the easy hike to its most significant ruin. Beyond that, it's possible to explore farther into the canyon as much as you like.

The trail starts in the stony wash next to the parking area. Descend the sandy bank and then follow the creek bed upcanyon to find an information board and trail register on the right.

The going is not easy on the route. Arch Canyon is a big canyon with a substantial drainage, collecting water from much of the east side of the Elk Ridge highlands. That water flows here and then pools in the canyon's low point in the wash, which the road crosses back and forth multiple times. In between, there are frequent pits of deep sand.

Sandstone formations above Arch Canyon.

Arch Canyon hoodoos.

The abundance of water also allows lush plant growth along the route, with large trees and thick reeds along the stream banks.

At 0.4 mile the trail emerges from the brush into an open area, with Arch Canyon Ruin perched on a broad, grassy knoll against the north wall (right when looking upcanyon).

A barb-wire fence runs the crest of the knoll. You can walk the length of the fence through the grass to inspect the ruin from a distance and get a general perspective on the site. A linked room block is the structure closest to the fence on the upcanyon end. At the far opposite (downcanyon) end, a gap in the fence allows you controlled access.

The canyon wall slopes gently over the site, but it is not sufficiently deep to create a true alcove. This leaves the south-facing structures to face the full brunt of the sun.

Arch Canyon Ruin and Trail

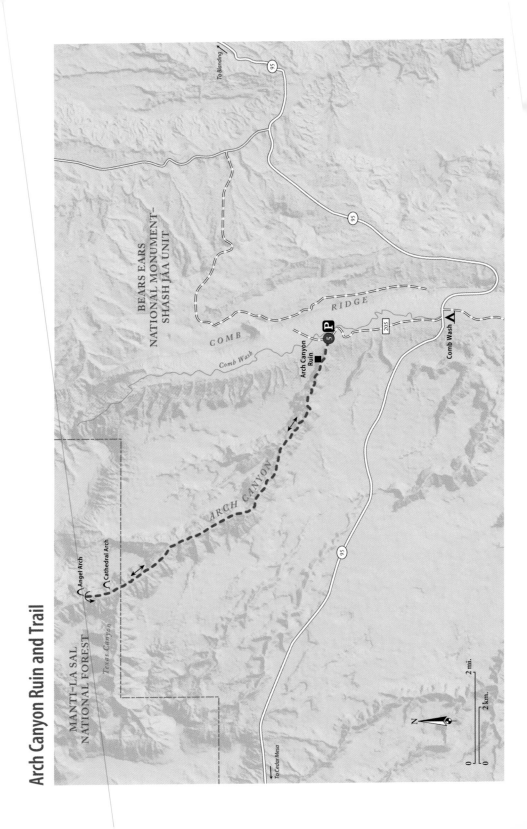

BEARS EARS
NATIONAL MONUMENT–
SHASH JÁA UNIT

COMB   RIDGE

Comb Wash

Arch Canyon Ruin

Comb Wash

ARCH CANYON

Angel Arch

Cathedral Arch

Texas Canyon

MANTI-LA SAL
NATIONAL FOREST

To Blanding

To Cedar Mesa

95

95

95

205

5 P

N

0   2 km.

0   2 mi.

Some of the still-standing wall remnants reach to a second story. You may investigate these structures, but be careful not to touch or otherwise harm any of the fragile and sometimes leaning walls. It wouldn't take much to bring these precarious towers toppling down.

The back wall of the canyon displays a host of petroglyphs, but they may require some effort to spot. There is little or no desert varnish on the red wall, so there is minimal contrast or color difference between the surface and the underlying, pecked-out rock.

Don't Touch Rock Imagery or Make Your Own

The petroglyphs consist mostly of abstract geometric designs interspersed with some more-recognizable snake and human-like shapes. A standard motif here is the spiral, which is common in rock art throughout the Bears Ears region. Some of the art is high and out of easy reach, possibly created by an artist standing on top of buildings that have since disappeared.

For most visitors, the trip to the ruin makes for a worthy outing by itself. But if you wish to explore further in Arch Canyon, the 4WD road continues for more than 12 miles through sculpted sandstone up toward its source on Elk Ridge. The only limit to how far you wish to go is your own imagination and endurance.

Unfortunately, seeing any of the arches for which the canyon is named requires a long outing, about 10 miles one way to the foot of Cathedral Arch. A better bet is to drive to Arch Canyon Overlook #1 instead, where you can see it from the rim.

Miles and Directions

0.0 Start at Arch Canyon Trailhead.

0.4 Reach Arch Canyon Ruin on the right (north).

3.5 Bypass north tributary junction on the right (north).

8.0 Bypass second north tributary junction on the right (north).

10.0 Bypass Texas Canyon junction on the left (west).

10.2 Reach Cathedral Arch on the right (east).

11.0 Reach Angel Arch on the right (east).

11.8 Reach Butts Canyon junction on the right (east).

Wall remnants at Arch Canyon Ruin.

Special precautions: Be sure to avoid trespassing on land owned by the Ute Reservation near the parking area and trailhead. This land is usually well signed.

Vehicle campsites: There are several dispersed car camping locations along SJC 205 between Arch Canyon Trailhead and UT 95. The more-developed Comb Wash Campsite lies directly across UT 95 from the SJC 205 junction with a lot of additional space. Amenities include latrines and picnic tables, but no water is available.

Mule Canyon Region

THE MULE CANYON COMPLEX CONSISTS OF A SYSTEM OF CANYONS running eastward down from Elk Ridge toward Comb Wash. These canyons boast an impressive array of Ancestral Puebloan archaeological sites with easy visitor access, including the famous House on Fire. Many are surface sites rather than cliff dwellings, and some are no farther away than a dedicated parking area alongside UT 95. This region also provides a jaw-dropping view into the depths of giant Arch Canyon from its rim and a trip up Salvation Knoll, a historic viewpoint used by the Hole-in-the-Rock Expedition of 1879.

Lower Mule Canyon from Cave Towers Ruin.

6 Cave Towers Ruin (Hike)

An easy hike to a rich collection of ancient structures on the rim of Mule Canyon.

Steer Clear of Walls

Start: Trailhead at the parking lot
Distance: 1 mile out and back to start of ruins
Elevation gain: 100 feet
Hiking time: 1–2 hours
Difficulty: Easy (short and flat)
Trail surface: Slickrock, sand, and dirt
Best season: Any time when dry
Other trail users: There may be 4x4s, ATVs, bikes, or horses on the trail (but not in ruins)
Canine compatibility: Leashed dogs allowed
Fees and permits: None
MAPS: USGS topo maps: Hotel Rock, Utah; **Other maps:** National Geographic Trails Illustrated #706, Grand Gulch Cedar Mesa Plateau
Trail contacts: Land owned by State of Utah School and Institutional Trust Lands Administration (SITLA), but most questions can be directed to BLM Monticello Field Office, 365 N. Main, PO Box 7, Monticello, UT 84535, (435) 587-1500, www.blm.gov/office/monticello-field-office; **Other (seasonal):** Kane Gulch Ranger Station, UT 261, 4 miles south of UT 95
Finding the trailhead: From the town of Blanding, take US 191 south for about 3 miles and turn right onto UT 95. Follow UT 95 west for 19 miles and look for a "Texas Flat Road/Mule Canyon" sign shortly before you reach milepost 102. Turn left (south) just past the sign onto a gated dirt road. Pass through the gate (close it behind you) and continue another 0.2 mile on a moderate dirt road to a large parking area.
GPS coordinates: N37° 31.93620' / W109° 43.93200'

The Hike

The cliff dwellings of Bears Ears are so pervasive that it is easy to forget how much archaeology sits on the mesa tops. However, most of the structures on the mesa tops have been directly exposed to the elements and

Surface structure at Cave Towers Ruin.

have collapsed or otherwise crumbled away. What remains is often only a raised dirt mound, unidentifiable as a ruin to the casual visitor.

Cave Towers is a nice exception to that rule. Here, a collection of seven ruins sits on the rim of Mule Canyon with a commanding view over the surrounding landscape. These are the "towers" of the name; for the "cave," look into the canyon, where additional structures are tucked into alcoves under the rim.

Start hiking down the road from the parking area. The trail starts to the right of the information board along the fence. Technically, this section of the road is still open to traffic, but it's rough enough that for many visitors it's almost as fast to walk as it would be to drive. Nonetheless, it is not unheard of for an ATV, 4x4, mountain bike, or equestrian to share the route with you.

After 0.4 mile, reach a second fence and information board detailing the site. This fence marks the end of the drivable section of the road, so all vehicles must stop here.

A few additional steps take you another 0.1 mile to the ruins and the end of the measured distance for the purpose of this hike. Beyond this point there is no set order for visiting the towers and no maintained trail to take you there, although you might find stretches of boot-beaten track or cairns to show you the way.

Despite the name, none of the towers is very high. Whatever upper levels that might once have existed have long since fallen away. Some of

Tower remnant with doorway.

the remaining structures are more complete than others; a stone ring with a still-visible "window" (actually a door) is easier to recognize as a tower than a linear wall and a pile of rubble. Some visitors will be challenged to even identify all seven structures.

The towers are clustered into two groups, with four on the left (east) side of Mule Canyon and three on the right (west). The dividing line between the groups is a slickrock pour-off above a green, leafy alcove. There is often water below the pour-off, protected by the shade of the overhanging rock. In a desert environment, building permanent settlements only makes sense near reliable water sources like this one.

That water source might have been so precious that it required protection. It's impossible not to stroll around the canyon rim without noticing the obvious advantages of this site as a defensive stronghold. No one could approach from below without being noticed when miles away. Even the term "towers" suggests fortification and security, bringing up images of guard towers and watchtowers.

Cave Towers is a particularly good site for binoculars, both to inspect the depths of Mule Canyon as well as the inaccessible shelves immediately below. A scan of the surrounding ledges and alcoves may reveal some interesting surprises, showing the true archaeological richness of the site. You can also investigate the sight lines between the ruins and wonder what significance, if any, there is to their particular orientations.

Although the towers have been stabilized to help prevent further deterioration, they are particularly fragile, so please do not enter or touch them.

Cave Towers Ruin

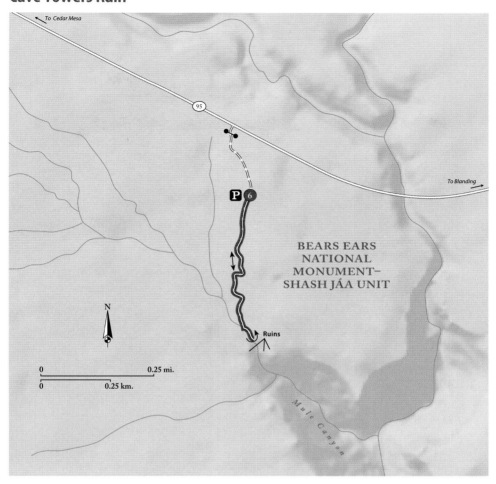

Miles and Directions

0.0 Start from trailhead at parking lot.

0.4 Reach second information board.

0.5 Reach ruin cluster.

1.0 End back at the trailhead.

Mountain bike opportunities: You can ride the short distance from the parking area to the end of the road and back, if that is preferable to walking.

7 Mule Canyon Kiva (Drivable Landmark)

An extensively restored archaeological site right off the highway.

Steer Clear of Walls

Visiting time: Up to 1 hour
Best season: Year-round
Canine compatibility: Leashed dogs allowed
Fees and permits: None
MAPS: USGS topo maps: South Long Point and Hotel Rock, Utah; **Other maps:** National Geographic Trails Illustrated #706, Grand Gulch Cedar Mesa Plateau
Contacts: BLM Monticello Field Office, 365 N. Main, PO Box 7, Monticello, UT 84535, (435) 587-1500, www.blm.gov/office/monticello-field-office; **Other (seasonal):** Kane Gulch Ranger Station, UT 261, 4 miles south of UT 95
Finding the trailhead: From the town of Blanding, take US 191 south for about 3 miles and turn right onto UT 95. Follow UT 95 west for 19.9 miles and turn right just short of milepost 101, signed for "Mule Canyon Ruins." Follow the paved road for about 0.1 mile to reach the circular parking area.
GPS coordinates: N37° 32.39760' / W109° 44.55180'

The Ruin

The name "Mule Canyon Kiva" undersells this site quite a bit. There is a lot more to see than just a kiva, and although it is adjacent to the Mule Canyon complex it is actually a surface site and not in Mule Canyon at all. But whatever the expectations, there is plenty here to explore.

Follow the short path from the east end of the parking area. This paved trail is just the first of many improvements that help make this site amenable to modern visitation.

Even before you reach the ruin you will notice the large sunshade that stands overhead, centered on the restored kiva. This sunshade mirrors many of the features of the kiva's original roof, now long gone. The modern vertical wood posts are similar to the original supports that once stood on the raised platforms (pilasters) around the kiva's wall. Wood slats lie on top of today's cross beams, similar to how logs or branches, typically

Mule Canyon Kiva.

juniper, would have rested on the original supports and then been sealed with dirt or clay.

The keyhole-shaped kiva was carefully stabilized and restored by the archaeological team that excavated it in the 1970s. It displays the typical layout and features of kivas from the Pueblo II and Pueblo III periods, when most of the structures at this site were built and put into use. The benches are complete, along with the pilasters, and a well-defined niche shows the fire pit and its protective deflection stone, rising out of the earthen floor.

Dogs & Archaeology Don't Mix

Note that there are actually two kivas at this site, although only one is visible. A second, more rudimentary kiva remains unrestored and under the ground. The simpler design of the second kiva means it likely predates the one on display.

Beyond the kivas the remnants of a series of rooms have also been stabilized and rebuilt to prevent further deterioration. These structures

Mule Canyon Kiva

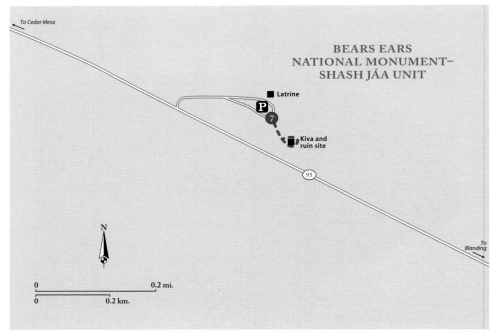

are linked together with common walls, like rooms in a motel, and are collectively called a room block.

The room block is laid out in an L-shaped orientation, common in both modern and ancient Pueblo architecture. The individual chambers would have been a mix of storage and living quarters, with access both via ladders from the roof and doorways opening onto the kiva plaza.

Look for the remnants of a circular tower standing alone to the east. A tunnel connects the tower to the kiva, and then a second tunnel leads to the nearest room. Look for the entrances to both these tunnels in the kiva's recessed niche.

Tunnels are an unusual feature in Ancestral Puebloan sites. Their connection to the kiva suggests they may have been used for ceremonial purposes, perhaps allowing someone to emerge in a surprise location for dramatic effect.

The tunnels may have also aided in defense, giving passage between the room block and the tower without being seen from the surface. The tower is thought to have stood two stories high, providing a sight line to the Cave Towers Ruin about a mile away across the highway, implying a linkage between the sites.

For more details on the ruin and its modern excavation, be sure to consult the display board adjacent to the site, which gives a great overview of its history and significance.

Surface roomblocks at Mule Canyon Kiva.

8 House on Fire Ruin (Hike)

A scenic canyon hike to a dramatic and well-known ruin.

Steer Clear of Walls

Start: South Fork Mule Canyon Trailhead
Distance: 2 miles out and back
Elevation gain: 100 feet
Hiking time: 1–2 hours
Difficulty: Easy (short and flat)
Trail surface: Sand, dirt, and rocks
Best season: Any time when dry
Canine compatibility: Leashed dogs allowed
Fees and permits: Cedar Mesa day-use permit required
MAPS: USGS topo maps: South Long Point and Hotel Rock, Utah; **Other maps:** National Geographic Trails Illustrated #706, Grand Gulch Cedar Mesa Plateau
Trail contacts: BLM Monticello Field Office, 365 N. Main, PO Box 7, Monticello, UT 84535, (435) 587-1500, www.blm.gov/office/monticello-field -office; **Other (seasonal):** Kane Gulch Ranger Station, UT 261, 4 miles south of UT 95
Finding the trailhead: From the town of Blanding, take US 191 south for about 3 miles and turn right onto UT 95. Follow UT 95 west for 19.4 miles and turn right (north) onto San Juan CR 263 (Texas Flat Road/Arch Canyon Road). At 0.3 mile, look for the trailhead on the left (west) side of the road where it crosses South Fork Mule Canyon. Park along the side of the road.
GPS coordinates: N37° 32.24760' / W109° 43.91580'

The Hike

The House on Fire might be the most famous archaeological site in Bears Ears. Pictures of it appear in all kinds of books and on numerous post-cards, although it is often unidentified. Chances are, you've already seen this ruin even if you didn't know it at the time.

There is good reason for it to get this kind of exposure. Not only is the House on Fire an excellent Ancestral Puebloan ruin in a "true canyon"

House on Fire Ruin.

setting, it's also easy to reach for just about any hiker. There are multiple easy-access sites in the vicinity of Mule Canyon, many with remarkable features, but the House on Fire still stands out.

South Fork Mule Canyon is itself an unusual canyon, to the hiker's benefit. Most canyons get deeper the farther they run, the end result of the accumulating effects of erosion. Here the hike accesses the bottom of the canyon, yet the depth is minimal.

The trail starts from the left (west) side of the road. Look for a gap in the brush marked with a post. The trail leads down to an information kiosk on the canyon floor and then swings upcanyon beneath some cottonwood trees.

The trail then meanders through a meadow before reaching the wash. Expect frequent crossings of the streambed as you make your way upcanyon, where the walls begin to narrow and deepen.

After 1 mile, watch carefully for a spur trail on the right, just before the canyon bends around a prominent point. Although the spur is well

House on Fire Ruin

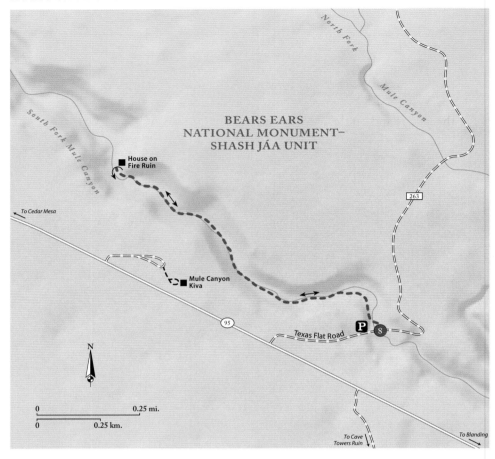

traveled and marked with a post, it can sometimes be obscured by brush. Follow the spur 20 feet uphill and emerge on a sandstone shelf, sloped upward to where the House on Fire is tucked against the wall.

Dogs & Archaeology Don't Mix

To find the famous view, continue around the bend a few more steps. From here the central rooms appear to be engulfed in flames, an illusion created by the banded layers of the overhanging sandstone. The effect is most pronounced if the canyon wall is lit by sunlight reflected from the floor, giving a reddish cast to the flames and making them appear to glow. The magnitude of the effect is influenced by the season, cloud cover, and time of day, but with a little luck you just might catch the ruin in full blaze.

The block of structures, although consisting of multiple, well-developed rooms, was likely used only for storage. These are granaries, not dwellings. Note the conspicuous absence of black charcoal stains on the interior of the rooms and on the canyon wall itself, indicators of habitual use of fires for cooking and heating and a telltale sign of habitation. Not only is the House on Fire not a house, there's also no evidence of actual fire.

It's easy to imagine the harm even a stone structure might incur if caught in the kind of inferno this site appears to be facing. Yet while the overhead flames are not real, this ruin is all too easy to damage in various other ways. Please do not enter any of the individual rooms or touch the buildings or walls. Sadly, you might be able to see stacks of loose stones in the bottom of some of the doorways. This rough reconstruction is an attempt to patch up structural damage caused by the cumulative effects of contact by well-meaning visitors.

Once your time at the ruin is complete, you can continue to explore up South Fork Mule Canyon on your own or else head back to your car.

Miles and Directions

0.0 Start at South Fork Mule Canyon Trailhead.

1.0 Reach the House on Fire Ruin.

2.0 End back at the trailhead.

9 Arch Canyon Overlook #1 (Drivable Landmark)

A jaw-dropping view into one of the deepest canyons on Cedar Mesa.

Stay on Designated Roads

Visiting time: Up to 1 hour
Best season: Any time when dry
Canine compatibility: Dogs allowed
Fees and permits: None
MAPS: USGS topo maps: South Long Point, Utah; **Other maps:** National Geographic Trails Illustrated #703, Manti-La Sal National Forest
Contacts: BLM Monticello Field Office, 365 N. Main, PO Box 7, Monticello, UT 84535, (435) 587-1500, www.blm.gov/office/monticello-field-office; **Other (seasonal):** Kane Gulch Ranger Station, UT 261, 4 miles south of UT 95
Finding the overlook: From the town of Blanding, take US 191 south for about 3 miles and turn right onto UT 95. Follow UT 95 west for 19.4 miles and turn right (north) onto San Juan CR (SJC) 263 (look for a sign for "Texas Flat Road/Mule Canyon"). Continue on SJC 263 for 6.1 miles and turn right onto an unmarked doubletrack. Follow the doubletrack for 0.2 mile to a small turnaround and parking area. See Description, below, for more details.
GPS coordinates: N37° 35.93934' / W109° 45.88740'

Description

Of the two overlooks into Arch Canyon, this one is the more impressive, looking into the deep chasm from a dizzying viewpoint on the rim. The cost of reaching this view is driving the approach road, which can be rough and tricky under normal conditions. However, the road is generally passable to standard 2WD cars and other vehicles, unless it is wet, when it should be avoided altogether.

The road to the overlook, San Juan CR 263, sometimes referred to as the Mule Canyon Road, Texas Flat Road, or Arch Canyon Overlook Road, is well traveled for the first mile where it provides access to the North and South Forks of Mule Canyon. Beyond that, it sees much fewer drivers.

The road crosses sand, rocks, dirt, and even a wash as it winds its way toward the viewpoint. People will typically be camped at pullouts along the way, often with trailers, RVs, and other large vehicles.

Cathedral Arch in Arch Canyon.

At 6.1 miles from the highway, turn right onto a rougher doubletrack road heading downhill. If you miss this turn, the road you are traveling on will soon deteriorate quickly, with deep ruts, sand, and tight brush on both sides. Should you encounter these difficulties, it's a good sign you've gone too far.

The side doubletrack on the right is also in considerably worse shape than the main access road. Luckily, if you are uncomfortable driving it, you can find a spot to park and walk the last 0.2 mile to the end. Note that there are often people camped in the area, so you may have to look for space.

When you reach the viewpoint, the yawning immensity of Arch Canyon suddenly opens before you. The canyon is nearly a mile across rim to rim from where you stand, 1,200 feet above the floor. Sheer sandstone walls run straight up and down, with little of the layered, "stair-stepped" look common to most Cedar Mesa canyons.

While standing on the rim of a canyon, it is often worth studying the notches, cracks, and ledges along the walls to see if you can find possible

Arch Canyon Overlook #1

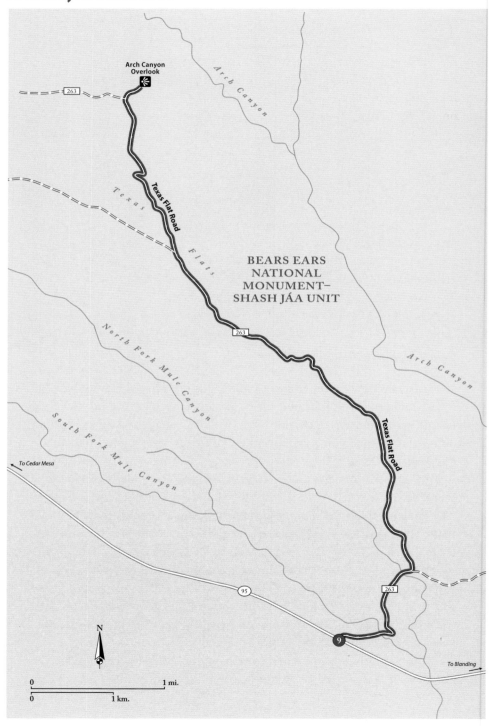

routes up or down. Often, a slide or other natural feature allows access—it "goes," in the common parlance. But you will be hard-pressed to find any such access route here, just sheer cliffs and drops.

The section of Arch Canyon you are viewing is just below the junction of three separate upcanyon forks. Texas Canyon is the one closest to you, followed by the main channel of Arch Canyon and then Butts Canyon on the right. You are standing on the edge of Texas Flat, so-named (along with the canyon) for the longhorns that ranchers used to run in this area. Butts Canyon is named for the Butt family, who have a long history in San Juan County. Their heritage stretches all the way back to brothers Parley and Willard "Dick" Butt, who arrived as part of the Hole-in-the-Rock Expedition in the late 1800s.

On the opposite wall it's easy to make out Cathedral Arch, the most prominent of the special features that give the canyon its name. A second arch, Angel Arch, stands farther to the left (northwest), but it is hidden among a collection of sandstone towers. There is also a giant alcove that looks like it might erode into an arch if given enough time, but you have arrived a few thousand years too soon.

Be sure to look for a set of metal stairs leading down to a slickrock promontory for the most panoramic view. Beyond the canyon itself, Ute Mountain and the Carrizo Mountains rise to the south along with the La Platas in Colorado to the east. You can also admire the deep clefts that Texas and Butts Canyons carve into the highlands of Elk Ridge, where they originate.

Suitability for mountain biking: There is no riding directly at the rim, but it is possible to ride San Juan CR 263 to and from the highway. Be sure to watch out for motor vehicle traffic on the rough road.

Vehicle campsites: Multiple informal campsites lie along the access road to the viewpoint, including several close to the rim of Arch Canyon. These campsites offer no services and do not require a permit.

Don't Build Fire Rings

10 Salvation Knoll (Hike)

A short climb to a commanding view, famously used by the Hole-in-the-Rock Expedition in 1879.

Stay on Designated Roads

Start: Trailhead at the parking pullout
Distance: 0.4 mile out and back
Elevation gain: 125 feet
Hiking time: Up to 1 hour
Difficulty: Easy (very short)
Trail surface: Packed dirt and rocks
Best season: Any time when dry
Canine compatibility: Dogs allowed
Fees and permits: None
MAPS: USGS topo maps: South Long Point, Utah; **Other maps:** National Geographic Trails Illustrated #706, Grand Gulch Cedar Mesa Plateau
Trail contacts: BLM Monticello Field Office, 365 N. Main, PO Box 7, Monticello, UT 84535, (435) 587-1500, www.blm.gov/office/monticello-field-office; **Other (seasonal):** Kane Gulch Ranger Station, UT 261, 4 miles south of UT 95
Finding the trailhead: From the town of Blanding, take US 191 south for about 3 miles and turn right onto UT 95. Follow UT 95 west for 24.3 miles to reach the parking pullout on the left, just short of milepost 97. There is room for only a few cars.
GPS coordinates: N37° 33.88440' / W109° 49.12020'

The Hike

In October 1879, a group of 250 Mormon pioneers set out from the town of Escalante, Utah, to establish a permanent settlement in the Four Corners region. They had no idea what they were getting into.

Expecting to be finished by mid-November, they ended up taking six months, struggling through some of the most rugged and forbidding terrain in North America. In the face of an unusually harsh winter, they had to negotiate a 200-mile maze of canyons, mesas, and mountains across the high desert.

Salvation Knoll view over Cedar Mesa.

The crux of the journey was the crossing of the Colorado River at what is now an upper reach of Lake Powell. The pioneers discovered a notch in the seemingly impenetrable canyon wall, unlocking a precipitous but viable descent to the river. The notch became known as the Hole-in-the-Rock, a name now given to the entire expedition.

For most of the journey, an advance team of scouts ranged far ahead of the main group of settlers, searching for the best route forward for their wagons and livestock. It was these scouts who climbed an unassuming hill on the northern edge of Cedar Mesa on Christmas Day 1879. Starving and desperate in the cold, the group trudged up through the snow to see the Abajo (Blue) Mountains less than 20 miles away to the northeast. This was the landmark they had been seeking, the signal that their epic ordeal was coming to an end.

Sensing they had been saved by divine providence, they named the hill Salvation Knoll.

Now you too can enjoy the same view—without any of the suffering. A short trail, built by descendants of the original settlers, wraps around the south side of the knoll to reach the top.

Salvation Knoll trail.

Although Elk Ridge blocks the vantage to the north, the trail still provides a commanding view with every step. On a clear day, you can see the Carrizo Mountains along the New Mexico/Arizona border to the southeast, Ute Mountain and the distant San Juan Mountains in Colorado to the east, lone Navajo Mountain in Arizona to the southwest, and the nearby Abajo Mountains in Utah. Directly at your feet, the eastern drainages of Cedar Mesa slant away toward Comb Ridge, including prominent Fish Creek Canyon.

Other than UT 95, which roughly follows the path established by the Hole-in-the-Rock pioneers, little evidence of human development is visible today. Imagine what it was like for the scouts to gaze out from this point in the winter of 1879. They studied the tortured landscape to determine a route across Cedar Mesa and around Comb Ridge, where they went on to found the towns of Bluff and Montezuma Creek.

They must have found the view a relief. But did they find it beautiful? In the face of their hardships, it's hard to say.

Look for display boards at the parking area, trailhead, and summit for more details about the Hole-in-the-Rock Expedition, now recognized as one of the greatest treks in American history.

Salvation Knoll

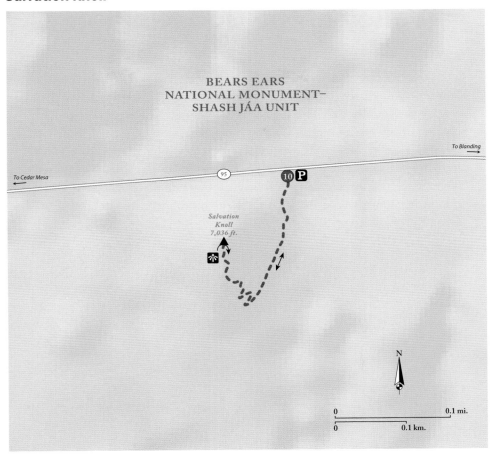

Miles and Directions

0.0 Start from the trailhead.

0.2 Reach the summit.

0.4 End back at the trailhead.

Valley of the Gods Region

VISITORS TO THE VALLEY OF THE GODS CAN EXPECT AN AWE-INSPIRING journey through soaring pinnacles of sandstone. Just as rewarding is a trip up the southern edge of Cedar Mesa, whose towering, multicolored cliffs form the valley's wall. Gazing out from the mesa's edge reveals a huge slice of vertical and geological relief, dropping thousands of feet into the serpentine depths of the San Juan River Canyon. No matter where you go in this region, remarkable views will be your reward, from the escarpment rim at Muley Point to the bottom of the Honaker Trail along the river's edge.

Valley of the Gods from the Moki Dugway.

11 Valley of the Gods (Scenic Drive)

An easy drive through a spectacular red-rock landscape of towering pinnacles, mesas, buttes, and canyons.

Stay on Designated Roads

Starting point: The junction of San Juan CR 242 (Valley of the Gods Road) and US 163. Note that Valley of the Gods can be driven in either direction but is described here from east to west.
GPS coordinates: N37° 14.09340' / W109° 48.85260'
Finding the start: From the town of Bluff, take Main Street/US 191 south for about 3.5 miles and then stay right at the intersection onto US 163 south toward Monument Valley. Continue on US 163 south for another 12.4 miles to a right turn onto a gravel road, across from milepost 29. The drive follows this gravel road, which is San Juan CR 242 (Valley of the Gods Road).
Total distance: 16.8 miles

Key Points

0.0 Start drive and cross cattle guard and Lime Creek wash.

2.9 Wrap around Setting Hen Butte.

5.9 Cross West Fork Lime Creek wash.

7.7 Reach high saddle at Castle Butte.

8.9 Cross large wash.

11.1 Cross large wash with hard gray rock surface.

13.0 Cross large wash.

16.3 Valley of the Gods Bed and Breakfast.

16.8 End at UT 261.

Time required: 1–2 hours, depending on how often you stop for photographs
Best season: Any time when dry
MAPS: USGS topo maps: Mexican Hat, Cigarette Spring Cave, and Cedar Mesa South, Utah; **Other maps:** National Geographic Trails Illustrated #706, Grand Gulch Cedar Mesa Plateau

Valley of the Gods

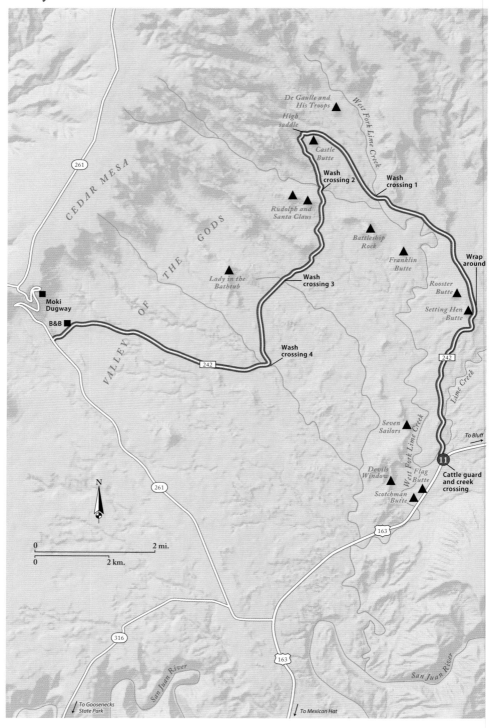

Contacts: BLM Monticello Field Office, 365 N. Main, PO Box 7, Monticello, UT 84535, (435) 587-1500, www.blm.gov/office/monticello-field-office; **Other (seasonal):** Kane Gulch Ranger Station, UT 261, 4 miles south of UT 95
Fees and permits: None
Minimum vehicle requirements: Any standard passenger car should be able to complete the drive when the road is dry.
Difficulty: Easy
Road conditions: This is a well-maintained gravel and dirt road with a few rough wash crossings and some washboarded sections. However, the road becomes impassable when wet.
Suitability for mountain biking: Although far from singletrack, this is a good nontechnical ride with some sustained climbs and descents. Expect to share the road with some vehicle traffic, including large RVs and campers. It can get very hot and dusty during the middle part of the day, and high winds are not unusual, especially in the afternoons. No water sources along the route.
Hiking: There are no maintained foot trails in Valley of the Gods.
Vehicle campsites: Multiple pullouts along the road allow for dispersed car camping with no permits required. Even during the busiest times, there is usually space available somewhere. No services are provided and no fires allowed.
Special attractions: The Valley of the Gods Bed and Breakfast provides visitors with a unique lodging experience on the site of the historic Lees Ranch. Reservations are required. Expect to meet other guests from around the world and see some spectacular sunsets.

The Drive

Like the more-famous Monument Valley along the Arizona/Utah border to the south, Valley of the Gods presents a signature western landscape. With its soaring spires and monoliths, Valley of the Gods is like Monument Valley's little brother: smaller, less visited, and less commercial. But the rock formations here are just as impressive as the ones there, iconic symbols of the American West.

To start the drive, turn right off US 163 onto the gravel Valley of the Gods Road. Immediately cross a cattle guard and then Lime Creek wash. There may be water in the wash during wet periods; if you're not sure your vehicle can safely make it across, then it's a good idea to turn around

Valley of the Gods from Cedar Mesa rim.

and come back another day. High water in Lime Creek can also indicate that other parts of the road are too wet to drive, so think carefully before proceeding.

Once across the wash, the road gradually climbs north on a broad bench between the two main valley drainages, Lime Creek on the right and its West Fork on the left. Be sure to take advantage of the frequent pullouts that line the road, useful for taking in the view and also as potential campsites.

Wrap around the east side of Setting Hen Butte after 2.9 miles and continue past Rooster Butte. Do the buttes match their names? It's easy to see the hen, particularly when viewed from the northeast, but the rooster seems to have been chosen for its symbolically masculine rather than avian features.

Continue north as Battleship Rock begins to dominate the view to the left (west) and the road crosses several washes. The largest of these crossings is West Fork Lime Creek at the 5.9-mile mark.

Beyond Battleship Rock you will enter the most visually impressive section of the valley, where the sandstone formations are most densely packed and you pass the mouths of several Cedar Mesa canyons. At 7.7 miles, reach a saddle behind Castle Butte, the highest point on the drive at 5,108 feet and a great place to stop and enjoy the view.

The second half of the drive starts with a switchback descent. For the next several miles you will generally face away from Cedar Mesa, allowing

Rooster and Sitting Hen Buttes.

distant views of the surrounding area. Look for the distinctive red and gray folds of Raplee Ridge to the south.

Once again you will cross several washes, including two large ones at 8.9 miles and 11.1 miles. The second is unusual for its hard gray rock surface, the top layer of a stratum known as the Rico Formation, which underlies much of the valley but is not often visible. After you have passed the Lady in the Bathtub, also known as the Balanced Rock, you will reach the final major wash crossing at about the 13-mile mark, where the road takes a broad turn to the right (west).

There were once several homesteads in the valley, but few traces remain. The exception is the Valley of the Gods Bed and Breakfast, on the site of the former Lees Ranch at 16.3 miles. The guesthouse draws visitors from around the world and is particularly popular with Europeans, who come for a desert experience unlike anything they can get at home. Despite its remote location, it is usually full.

Historic Artifacts Aren't Trash

Another 0.5 mile will bring you to the end of the drive at UT 261. Conveniently, you are at the foot of the Moki Dugway if you wish to continue your driving adventure.

12 Goosenecks State Park (Drivable Landmark)

The best place to view the massive entrenched meanders of the San Juan River Canyon.

Pay Your Fees

Visiting time: Up to 1 hour
Best season: Year-round
Canine compatibility: Dogs allowed
Fees and permits: Park entrance fee required
MAPS: USGS topo maps: The Goosenecks, Utah; **Other maps:** National Geographic Trails Illustrated #706, Grand Gulch Cedar Mesa Plateau
Contacts: Utah State Parks, https://stateparks.utah.gov/parks/goosenecks/discover/; **Other:** For information, contact the Edge of the Cedars State Park Museum in Blanding at (435) 678-2238.
Finding Goosenecks State Park: From the town of Bluff, take Main Street/US 191 south for about 3.5 miles and then stay right at the intersection onto US 163 south toward Monument Valley. Continue on US 163 south for another 16.6 miles to a right (north) turn onto UT 261. Follow UT 261 for 0.9 mile and turn left onto UT 316 toward Goosenecks State Park. Follow UT 316 for 3.5 miles to where it ends.
GPS coordinates: N37° 10.46520' / W109° 55.61400'

Description

Goosenecks State Park provides the best view of the San Juan River Canyon at its most impressive point, where the river twists back on itself multiple times through several oxbow bends, 1,000 feet deep.

As you gaze into the canyon, you are looking into the distant past. Around 300 million years ago, the river flowed across a broad plain, taking lazy, wandering turns as it went. Then, about 80 million years ago, the Colorado Plateau began to rise.

As the land went up, the river began to flow faster and erode the underlying rock, locking itself into its own channel. There was nowhere to go but down.

The end result is the canyon visible today, characterized by two main rock formations. The upper two-thirds of the canyon are made up of the

The Goosenecks from the overlook.

Honaker Trail Formation (or just Honaker Formation) with alternating layers of limestone and shale. This formation dates from 270 to 300 million years ago and is rich in fossilized marine life. The alternating layers of shale and limestone can be identified by their differing resistances to erosion. The softer shales form the loose-looking, disintegrating slopes between the horizontal cliff bands of the much harder limestone layers.

The bottom third of the canyon is made up of the limestone Paradox Formation, from between 310 and 300 million years ago. The ages of these rocks can be devoid of meaning; the Paradox Formation at 310 million years old doesn't seem much different from the Honaker Trail Formation at 300 million years old. Yet in between them lies *10 million years*, a period of time vastly beyond any human reference or scale, against which the entire history of civilization is little more than a rounding error. And that says nothing of the time between then and now, 30 times longer.

During the high flow of spring and summer, you may see the colorful kayaks and rafts of river runners on the water. If so, you can observe their passage through The Goosenecks, disappearing from sight for a while and then reappearing on the far side of each meander. Their slow journey through the canyon helps emphasize the winding path of the river, which flows a distance of more than 6 miles to cover a net east–west distance of less than 1.5 miles.

The best view of The Goosenecks is available from the main parking lot, but an alternate view is also available. An old, rough road from the east side of the lot leads out to a promontory point. This road runs about 1 mile, quickly deteriorating as it goes. The rough, rocky surface is best hiked or mountain biked; it's not worth driving.

Gooseenecks State Park

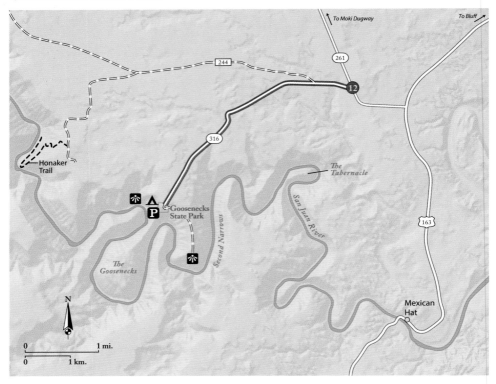

At the end, you can look over to the east at a section of river known as the Second Narrows, not visible from the main overlook. You can also look down on the river where it first enters The Gooseenecks, although without the kind of panoramic view you had before.

The drive to the park is entirely on paved roads, and the park itself provides a pit toilet, camping area, and picnic tables. This is a great place to stop for lunch and take in the view. If you are at The Gooseenecks for a picnic or other short visit, the quick hike to the alternate viewpoint makes a good way to stretch your legs and get a different perspective on this geologic wonder.

Special precautions: Although the park is open all year, the road can be covered by snow for short periods in the winter and the park can be brutally hot at midday in the summer.

Vehicle campsites: Camping is available at the park for a fee on a first-come, first-served basis.

13 Honaker Trail (Hike)

A steep descent through layers of ancient limestone and shale to the San Juan River.

Stay on Designated Roads

Start: Honaker Trailhead
Distance: 4.8 miles out and back
Elevation gain: 1,200 feet, mostly on return
Hiking time: 2–4 hours
Difficulty: Moderate to difficult, due to steepness, exposure, and heat
Trail surface: Dirt and rock
Best season: Any time when dry
Canine compatibility: Dogs allowed
Fees and permits: None
MAPS: USGS topo maps: The Goosenecks, Utah; **Other maps:** National Geographic Trails Illustrated #706, Grand Gulch Cedar Mesa Plateau
Trail contacts: BLM Monticello Field Office, 365 N. Main, PO Box 7, Monticello, UT 84535, (435) 587-1500, www.blm.gov/office/monticello-field -office; **Other (seasonal):** Kane Gulch Ranger Station, UT 261, 4 miles south of UT 95
Finding the trailhead: From the town of Bluff, take Main Street/US 191 south for about 3.5 miles and then stay right at the intersection onto US 163 south toward Monument Valley. Continue on US 163 south for another 16.6 miles to a right (north) turn onto UT 261. Follow UT 261 for 0.9 mile and turn left onto UT 316 toward Goosenecks State Park. In 0.5 mile turn right onto unmarked gravel San Juan CR 244. After 2.6 miles, stay left where the road forks at an old water tank. Continue on this road for another 1.9 miles and look for a rougher road on the right, which is the trailhead, usually marked with cairns. Park in the open space nearby. The road over the last 1.9 miles is usually passable to standard 2WD vehicles when dry, but if it becomes too rough you can park alongside the road and walk the rest of the way. There is a rocky arroyo crossing at about 1 mile that has a good parking pullout often used for this purpose.
GPS coordinates: N37° 11.31600' / W109° 57.06000'

The Hike

The Honaker Trail descends a different kind of canyon from most in the Bears Ears region. If the sandstone canyons of Cedar Mesa are a grand palace, the Honaker Trail is the cellar, penetrating deep layers of bedrock to reach the San Juan River at the bottom.

The trail is named for brothers Augustus and Henry Honaker, who held a placer claim along the river at the end of the nineteenth century. The trail roughly follows the historic route they used to access their claim, although in some sections they had to lower gear and even themselves by rope.

Historic Artifacts Aren't Trash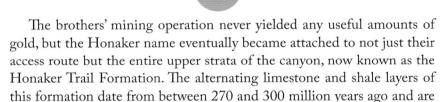

The brothers' mining operation never yielded any useful amounts of gold, but the Honaker name eventually became attached to not just their access route but the entire upper strata of the canyon, now known as the Honaker Trail Formation. The alternating limestone and shale layers of this formation date from between 270 and 300 million years ago and are noted for their ancient marine fossils.

The ideal time to hike the Honaker Trail is early in the morning, when the east wall is still in shadow. The shade is doubly important on the return, so it takes a very early start to ensure that you can climb out before the sun fully crests the rim, usually around 11 a.m.

The trail starts on the right (west) side of the access road, usually marked with a pair of cairns. Watch for this point carefully, as the road continues past the entrance for another 0.5 mile before it ends. The canyon rim lies about another 200 yards back from the start, marked with another cairn, several feet high. Look for this cairn from the road to help you find the correct starting place.

From the cairn, some steps carved into the rock mark the beginning of the descent. Head through some switchbacks and then enter the first of several long traverses, following the canyon wall to the southwest. The trail drops down through several small ledges and cliff bands as it goes. You may notice some numbers painted in yellow along the way, remnants of a geologic survey from years past.

The rocks here are sharp and pointy, very different from the sculpted sandstone higher up. Although there are some reddish bands, the prevailing

The San Juan River at the bottom of the Honaker Trail.

color is gray, and the walls can appear particularly washed out under the full light of the sun.

At 1.2 miles, reach a promontory point, known as the The Horn, which provides a view upriver and access to a cliff-defeating crack. The rock around The Horn is rich in fossilized brachiopods, visible along the trail with a careful search.

Don't Disturb Fossils or Bones

Drop down through the crevice and then follow another long traverse back to the northeast, contouring past the starting point at the rim. Once through the crack, you have left the rock layers of the Honaker Trail Formation and entered the even deeper layers of the Paradox Formation, dating from 300 to 310 million years ago.

The long traverses are necessary to connect the only available vulnerabilities in the formidable cliff bands. These traverses can grow tedious on the descent; you will be running parallel to the San Juan for long stretches

The San Juan River Canyon from the rim.

without getting any closer. But you might feel differently about them on the way out, when they provide a welcome break between sections of hard climbing.

A third long traverse brings you to the last downward section and then finally the bank of the river. Just as at the top, the end of the trail is marked with a large cairn. The elevation at the river is just under 4,000 feet, one of the lowest points anywhere in Bears Ears.

A river runner's campsite about 100 yards upstream offers the easiest way to reach the silty water. If you are tempted to take a dip, use plenty of caution; the water runs much faster and colder than you'd think.

From the bottom of the canyon, the cliffs above look insurmountable, despite the fact that's where you just came down. On the hike back out, the great effort and care that went into building the trail is laid bare. Many of the trail sections that seem to follow

Shadows and rock layers along the Honaker Trail.

Honaker Trail

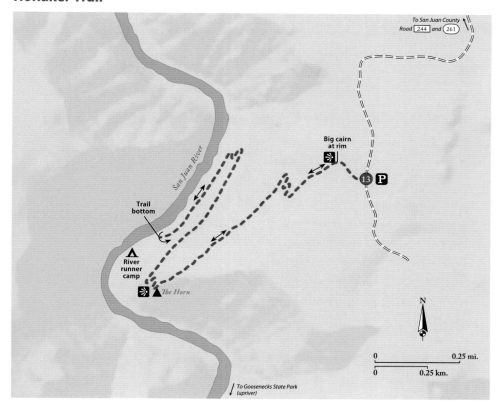

the natural lay of the land were actually built by human hands. Look for multiple ramps and restraining walls of stacked rocks that stabilize the ground and make possible your passage through this demanding terrain.

Miles and Directions

0.0 Start from the trailhead.

0.1 Reach the big cairn on the canyon rim.

1.2 Reach The Horn rock formation.

2.4 Reach the San Juan River.

4.8 End back at the trailhead.

Special precautions: There is some exposure on this trail, so it may not be suitable for children or anyone with a fear of cliffs or heights. It can also get very hot, due to low elevation and no shade after early morning.

14 Moki Dugway (Scenic Drive)

A short road climb with some stunning views up the southern face of Cedar Mesa.

Stay on Designated Roads

Starting point: UT 261, 7.5 miles north of the junction with US 163. Note that the Moki Dugway can be driven in either direction, but is described here going uphill.
GPS coordinates: N37° 16.34160' / W109° 56.65440'
Finding the start: From the town of Bluff, take Main Street/US 191 south for about 3.5 miles and then stay right at the intersection onto US 163 south toward Monument Valley. Continue on US 163 south for another 16.6 miles to a right (north) turn onto UT 261. The Dugway is on UT 261, 7.5 miles away.
Total distance: 2.5 miles

Key Points

0.0 Start where pavement ends at first switchback.

0.5 Left turn around point.

0.8 Switchback to the left.

1.0 Switchback to the right.

1.5 Switchback to the left.

2.0 Fenced viewpoint at switchback to the right.

2.5 End where pavement restarts and road levels off.

Time required: Up to 1 hour
Best season: Year-round
MAPS: USGS topo maps: Cedar Mesa South, Utah; **Other maps:** National Geographic Trails Illustrated #706, Grand Gulch Cedar Mesa Plateau
Contacts: BLM Monticello Field Office, 365 N. Main, PO Box 7, Monticello, UT 84535, (435) 587-1500, www.blm.gov/office/monticello-field-office; **Other (seasonal):** Kane Gulch Ranger Station, UT 261, 4 miles south of UT 95
Fees and permits: None
Minimum vehicle requirements: Not recommended for trucks over 10,000 pounds GVW, RVs, buses, or vehicles with trailers, owing to 10 percent

Moki Dugway

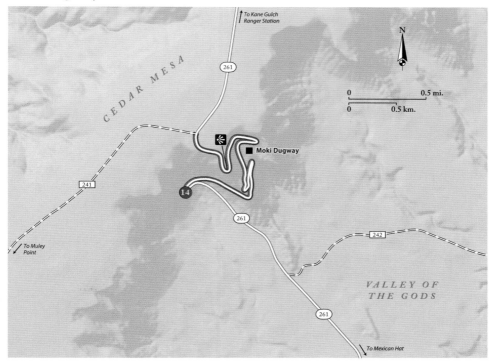

gradients and sharp turns. Any standard passenger car should be able to complete the drive.

Difficulty: Easy

Road conditions: This is a well-maintained gravel and dirt road with some washboarded sections.

Suitability for mountain biking: The Dugway is open to mountain bikes but not recommended. This is either a grueling grind straight uphill or a brake-melting descent straight down, with potential motor vehicle traffic to dodge around the blind turns.

Vehicle campsites: Dispersed car camping is available in Valley of the Gods, just southeast of the Dugway.

The Drive

Despite all the canyons, mesas, and mountains spread out across the Bears Ears region, some people visit just to drive the Moki Dugway. Nowhere else can you get so much reward for so little effort.

The Moki Dugway is the crux of UT 261, which runs south from UT 95 across Cedar Mesa to US 163 near Mexican Hat. The total distance is 33 miles, with a cumulative descent of about 2,000 feet. Half of that descent takes place in the 2.5 miles of the Dugway.

UT 261 was built in 1956 to service a uranium mine in White Canyon, in the area of present-day Natural Bridges National Monument. In 1957 the mining company donated the road to the State of Utah, who paved its entire length over the next twenty years—with the exception of the Dugway. It may have been that the costs of paving the Dugway far outweighed the benefits, but local lore holds that the gravel surface was kept in order to discourage people from driving the road too fast. Near the top it's possible to find the rusted wreckage of what appears to be a vehicle that slid over the edge, with disastrous consequences.

Moki Dugway climbing up Cedar Mesa.

Historic Artifacts Aren't Trash

As you approach the Dugway from the south, multiple signs warn you of what is to come: 10 percent grades and narrow switchbacks, making the road unsuitable for the largest vehicles. But you will be amazed that any road lies ahead at all; the face of Cedar Mesa appears to be an impregnable wall. Even when you are right at the foot of the Dugway, it will look like you are about to drive straight up a cliff.

The pavement ends at the first switchback, 7.5 miles from US 163. Looking up from the bottom, all the rock layers of Cedar Mesa are exposed before you. Note the transition from the red sandstone at the base to the lighter yellows at the rim. These colors together make up what is collectively known as the Cedar Mesa Sandstone.

It pays to proceed cautiously up the climb. Be particularly careful if you stop and get out along the way, since blind curves make you difficult to see and there is no shoulder to speak of. Other vehicles, even when driving slowly, are unlikely to be following the stated speed limit of 5 mph around the turns. Your best bet for enjoying the view is at the designated viewpoint, just below the top.

When you reach the viewpoint, be sure to walk the length of the guardrail to take in the entire scene. The buttes and hoodoos of Valley of the Gods lie to the left (northeast) and are echoed farther away to the right (south) by the larger formations in Monument Valley. In between, Bell Butte, Raplee Ridge, and Alhambra Rock lead the way down to the town of Mexican Hat and the San Juan River Canyon. Look below for other vehicles snaking their way through the Dugway's twists and turns.

From the top, you can head back down the way you came for a different perspective on the same landscape. You could also head to nearby Muley Point for another spectacular view off Cedar Mesa's southern edge. Finally, you could continue north on UT 261 across the top of Cedar Mesa, riding the uppermost band of all those layers of multicolored rock you have just climbed through.

15 Muley Point Lookout (Drivable Landmark)

A celebrated overlook with a signature canyon-country view.

Stay on Designated Roads

Visiting time: Up to 1 hour
Best season: Any time when dry
Canine compatibility: Dogs allowed
Fees and permits: None
MAPS: USGS topo maps: The Goosenecks, Utah; **Other maps:** National
Geographic Trails Illustrated #706, Grand Gulch Cedar Mesa Plateau
Contacts: Muley Point is officially part of Glen Canyon National Recreation
Area: GCRA, PO Box 1507, Page, AZ 86040, (928) 608-6200. However, the
BLM can usually answer any questions you might have: BLM Monticello
Field Office, 365 N. Main, PO Box 7, Monticello, UT 84535, (435) 587-1500,
www.blm.gov/office/monticello-field-office. **Other (seasonal):** Kane Gulch
Ranger Station, UT 261, 4 miles south of UT 95
Finding Muley Point: From the town of Bluff, take Main Street/US 191 south
for about 3.5 miles and then stay right at the intersection onto US 163 south
toward Monument Valley. Continue on US 163 south for another 16.6 miles
to a right (north) turn onto UT 261. Follow UT 261 for 10 miles up the Moki
Dugway. At the top of the Dugway, turn left onto San Juan CR 241. Follow
this road for 5.1 miles to where it ends.
GPS coordinates: N37° 13.99080' / W109° 59.57460'

Description

Local legend holds that Muley Point was Edward Abbey's favorite spot in
the Southwest. Whether that is true or not, this viewpoint on the southern edge of Cedar Mesa is the kind of place that Abbey both celebrated
in his writing yet somehow hoped to keep from public attention.

After parking your car, make your way across the slickrock to take it
all in. At 6,200 feet, Muley Point has an edge-of-the-world vibe similar
to the view at the Grand Canyon, although smaller in scale.

A wide outer rift fills most of the scene with an impressive display of
exposed strata. The northern wall of this rift is the Cedar Mesa escarpment

Looking west from Muley Point.

and its floor is the broad bench below. Look for an obvious dirt road that runs across this bench, winding its way around the heads of multiple short draws. Known as the E. L. Goodridge Road or the Johns Canyon Road, it was built by an ambitious local prospector named E. L. Goodridge in 1908 to access an oil well he was developing at the mouth of Slickhorn Canyon, about 12 miles to the northwest (on your right).

Unfortunately for Goodridge, his drilling equipment tumbled off a cliff before he was able to extract a single drop of oil. The road still remains, however, and is used by ranchers and others to access Johns Canyon, the closest Cedar Mesa canyon to where you stand.

Below the road, the inner gorge of the San Juan River cuts its way through the bench with another impressive geological display. The gorge is only about 1 horizontal mile distant, but it's so steep and narrow that the river itself is hard to see.

However, with a little searching you can find a few spots where the silty water is revealed at the bottom of the gorge's oxbow bends. The surface of the river sits at an elevation of about 3,600 feet, 2,600 feet below.

Muley Point Lookout

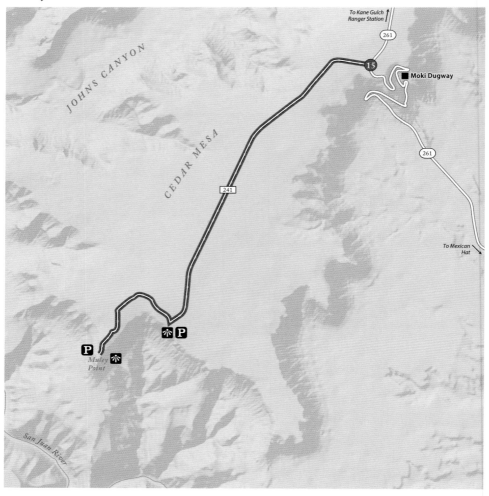

The far side of the San Juan belongs to the Navajo Nation, starting with Douglas Mesa, which forms the opposite wall of the outer canyon. The hoodoos of Monument Valley rise to the south, with the angular monolith of Agathla Rock and the coal-rich bulk of Black Mesa, near the town of Kayenta, Arizona, visible beyond.

Navajo Mountain (*Naatsis'áán* to Navajo speakers) crowns the western horizon, climbing to 10,346 feet and often snowcapped even in summer. This is one of the four sacred mountains that mark the boundary of the traditional Navajo homeland and still roughly define the Navajo

Muley Point view to Monument Valley.

Reservation today. The upper reaches of Lake Powell on the Colorado River sit at the mountain's north foot, but they are hidden from here.

The distant Henry Mountains stand on the northwest horizon, 11,552 feet at their highest point. The Henrys are so remote that they were the last mountain range in the contiguous 48 states to be mapped and named.

Behind you, a string of prominent buttes parades across the landscape, including Bears Ears, Moss Back, and the Tables of the Sun. From Muley Point they are blocked by the intervening slopes of Cedar Mesa, but you might catch a glimpse of them on the drive out.

Special precautions: If your vehicle is unable to drive up the Moki Dugway, you will need to approach from the north side of Cedar Mesa via UT 95 and then UT 261 south. San Juan CR (SJC) 241 may be impassable when wet. Note that there is a popular viewpoint at mile 3.8 on SJC 241 with space for a lot of cars, but the true Muley Point is 1.3 miles farther along.

Vehicle campsites: Dispersed car camping is available anywhere on the top of Cedar Mesa with no fee or permit required, including right at Muley Point. However, high winds are common near the rim and sometimes carry a nasty payload of sand and grit.

Don't Build Fire Rings

Grand Gulch/Cedar Mesa Canyons Region

CEDAR MESA IS THE CROWN JEWEL OF BEARS EARS, AND GRAND GULCH and its tributary canyons are the crown jewels of Cedar Mesa. The trips in this region explore these magical canyons, but every destination must be earned. This is the best region for hikers; every trip here requires you to get out of your car and travel on foot. In return, expect a scenic payoff around every corner: epic canyons, majestic rock formations, and archaeological wonders. The trips detailed here are some of the longest in this guide, including two multiday backpacks, but chances are you'll wish they were longer.

Grand Gulch.

Kane Gulch Trail

16 Junction Ruin (Hike)
17 Turkey Pen Ruin (Hike)
18 Split Level Ruin (Backpack)

The Kane Gulch Trail is the best route into the heart of Grand Gulch, leading to the greatest concentration of significant archaeological sites anywhere in Bears Ears.

Start: Trailhead at Kane Gulch Ranger Station
Distance:
  Junction Ruin: 8.2 miles out and back
  Turkey Pen Ruin: 10.2 miles out and back
  Split Level Ruin: 20.6 miles out and back
Elevation gain:
  Junction Ruin: 600 feet, mostly on return
  Turkey Pen Ruin: 620 feet, mostly on return
  Split Level Ruin: 900 feet, mostly on return
Hiking time:
  Junction Ruin: 5–7 hours
  Turkey Pen Ruin: 6–9 hours
  Split Level Ruin: 2–3 days
Difficulty:
  Junction Ruin: Moderate, due to length and some route-finding
  Turkey Pen Ruin: Moderate to difficult, due to length and some route-finding
  Split Level Ruin: Difficult, due to length and some route-finding
Trail surface: Sand, dirt, and rocks
Best season: Spring and fall
Canine compatibility: No dogs allowed
Fees and permits: Cedar Mesa day-use or backpacking permit required
MAPS: USGS topo maps: Kane Gulch, Utah, for Junction Ruin and Turkey Pen Ruin; add Cedar Mesa North for Split Level Ruin; **Other maps:** National Geographic Trails Illustrated #706, Grand Gulch Cedar Mesa Plateau
Trail contacts: BLM Monticello Field Office, 365 N. Main, PO Box 7, Monticello, UT 84535, (435) 587-1500, www.blm.gov/office/monticello-field-office; **Other (seasonal):** Kane Gulch Ranger Station, UT 261, 4 miles south of UT 95

Kane Gulch Trail: Junction Ruin, Turkey Pen Ruin, Split Level Ruin

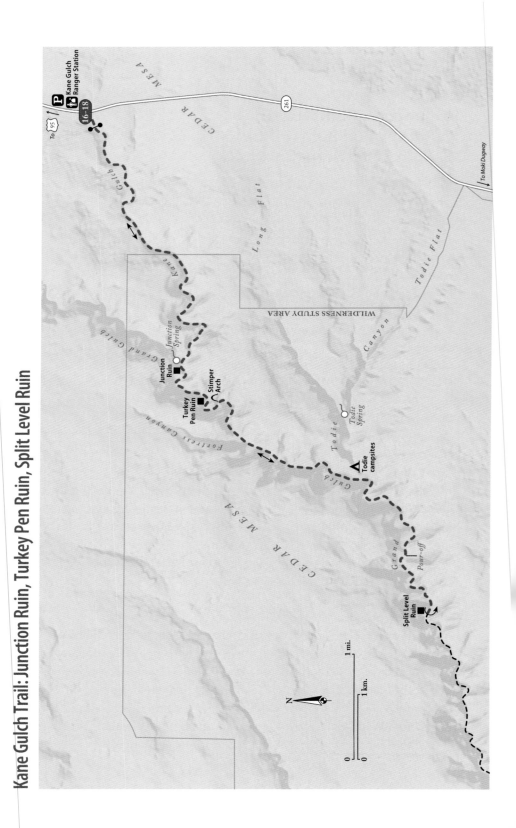

Finding the trailhead: From the town of Blanding, take US 191 south for about 3 miles and turn right onto UT 95. Follow UT 95 west for 28.4 miles and turn left (south) onto UT 261. Go 3.9 miles on UT 261 and park at Kane Gulch Ranger Station on the left.

GPS coordinates: N37° 31.47600' / W109° 53.76780'

The Hikes

The three archaeological sites described here are all in the same canyon and on the same trail. Junction Ruin is the first significant destination available to day hikers and the easiest option from the trailhead. Turkey Pen Ruin lies another mile beyond, somewhat more difficult due to the additional distance. Split Level Ruin is substantially farther, best suited for backpackers who plan on spending one or two nights in the canyon.

16 Junction Ruin (Hike)

Steer Clear of Walls

The Kane Gulch Trail starts on the far side of UT 261 from the ranger station. Look for an information board and gap in the fence on the west side of the parking lot and then carefully cross the roadway to begin your hike.

High ledge at Junction Ruin.

Vertical posts and ladder remnant at Junction Ruin.

Pass through a cattle gate at 0.1 mile as the trail winds in and out of Kane Creek. Brush lines the stream banks and canyon walls, with reeds near the wash and sagebrush farther up. Aspens and other high-elevation trees grow here as well.

Cairns mark the way for much of the descent. At 2.1 miles a sign indicates you are entering the Grand Gulch Wilderness Study Area. Several small pour-offs and jumbled boulders blocking the wash must be avoided over the next 0.5 mile. Below the pour-offs the canyon takes a sharp turn to the left and the walls become noticeably deeper.

Some additional twists bring you to the junction with the main channel of Grand Gulch, at 4.1 miles. A reliable spring provides water to multiple campsites and a grove of cottonwoods at the confluence. The spring was also the water source used by the ancient inhabitants of Junction Ruin, which sits in a huge amphitheater on the north wall.

The ruin consists of three separate layers, spaced sufficiently far apart that some effort is required to see them all. The top two layers, especially the highest, are best viewed from a distance. Some structures on the highest ledge are recessed far enough in the alcove that they are hidden if viewed from directly below.

Enjoy Archaeology Without Ropes

The topmost layer is marked by a series of vertical wooden posts at the far left end, next to the remnants of a ladder. Even with the ladder intact, the ascent up the sheer sandstone wall must have been harrowing.

The base of the ladder would have been anchored at the rudimentary wall structure on the small ledge below, the middle layer of the ruin.

Unlike the top two layers, the lowest layer is easily accessible on foot. Be sure to mind the chains protecting the midden area in front of the large alcove. You may otherwise explore the ruins here, taking care not to stand on or lean against any walls. Two separate kivas are worthy of special attention.

Some pictographs grace the rear wall of the alcove, including mud daubs, handprints, and some heavily faded yellow anthropomorphs that require the right light and a certain viewing angle to see. Consult the information in the ammo box provided by the BLM at the far left end of the ruin for more details on the site.

Don't Touch Rock Imagery or Make Your Own

17 Turkey Pen Ruin (Hike)

Turkey Pen Ruin lies another mile down Grand Gulch from Junction Ruin. Although this only adds 2 miles round-trip, be sure to budget enough time for both the extra hike and exploration of the site if you plan to visit.

To reach Junction Ruin, you hiked down Kane Gulch, a Grand Gulch tributary. Below Junction Ruin you are now in the main channel of Grand Gulch, where towering sandstone walls drop straight to the canyon floor, the trail winds in and out of the wash through brush and cottonwoods, and the downcanyon descent is so shallow that it feels essentially flat.

There is no officially maintained trail here, but for the most part the traveling is easy. As you make your way downcanyon, keep your eyes peeled for additional rock art and ruins all around. Archaeological sites may be tucked under the rim far above, on airy ledges partway up the walls, or down near the canyon floor where you are hiking. Some may appear behind you and be easier to see on the return.

The giant Turkey Pen alcove.

Stimper Arch.

At 5 miles from the trailhead (0.9 mile below Junction Ruin), pass through some oxbow meanders. Despite the height of the canyon walls, you can expect very little shade here during the heat of the day.

At 5.1 miles, look for the massive Turkey Pen alcove on the right, facing south (downcanyon). Entrance to the site is from the east end, near a BLM ammo box of information.

Feel free to carefully explore the ruins, but always be respectful of the fragility of these structures. Stay behind the chains to protect the midden and other highly sensitive areas.

Steer Clear of Walls

Look for a ring of vertical sticks, an enclosure resembling a pen for domesticated turkeys, for which the ruin is named. This unusual feature is lucky to have remained standing, since the site was abandoned at the end of the thirteenth century. Turkeys were raised and kept by the Ancestral Puebloans as a source for feathers for blankets and no doubt as an occasional food source as well.

Structure remnants at Turkey Pen Ruin.

Charcoal stains on the alcove's back wall show where additional structures once stood, the black marks left over from fires burned in the interiors of now-absent rooms. Also on the back wall is a collection of rock art, with a mix of some pictographs and a few faint petroglyphs.

Don't Touch Rock Imagery or Make Your Own

The enclosure that gives Turkey Pen Ruin its name.

The Turkey Pen alcove lies directly across the canyon from the wall fin that hosts Stimper Arch. However, the arch is not readily visible from the upcanyon side. To view the arch, head downcanyon for another 0.4 mile to wrap around the fin and look for the opening high in the sandstone wall.

18 Split Level Ruin (Backpack)

Camp & Eat Away from Archaeology

Below Stimper Arch, route-finding can sometimes be a challenge, as multiple tracks present themselves, and it is up to the individual to determine the best way to go. The trail frequently crosses the wash, often to take the inside or outside track around bends in the canyon. Sometimes the trail runs on high benches above the wash and other times it drops sharply in and out of the wash through steep, sandy notches.

At 6.1 miles from the trailhead (1 mile below Turkey Pen), the tributary of Fortress Canyon enters from the north (right looking downcanyon). A smaller box canyon tributary enters from the same side in another 0.5 mile.

Anthropomorph and main structures at Split Level Ruin.

Some campsites appear on the benches on either side of the wash, but they are generally devoid of water. The best camping option for backpackers is at Todie Canyon, 7.5 miles down from the trailhead. Todie enters Grand Gulch from the east side (left looking downcanyon), marked by a prominent sandstone fin projecting out into the main channel.

There are multiple good campsites in the bottom of Todie, served by a reliable spring. Water is usually available about a quarter mile upcanyon, although in drier times it may be necessary to venture farther up Todie to find it.

Todie makes a good base camp for adventure for a multiday backpacking trip. From here it's easy to make a day trip out and back to Split Level Ruin. On a two-day itinerary, the journey would have to be added to either the entrance or exit days, although it could be completed without carrying full gear. On a three-day itinerary, camping at Todie allows an easy day trip to Split Level Ruin on the middle day, generally with plenty of time to explore Todie Canyon as well.

Past Todie the way becomes noticeably rougher, with much less foot traffic. The benches above the wash are often overgrown with grasses and brush, while the wash may be no better, with sections choked with flash flood debris. Whatever speed you made on the upper part of the trail is likely to decline here.

Nonetheless, this is the most magical section of the hike, where seemingly every twist in the canyon reveals another soaring alcove and another archaeological treasure.

GPS Reveals Too Much

At 9 miles from the trailhead (1.5 miles below Todie Canyon), a large pour-off impedes your path, requiring a bypass on the south (left) side. This pour-off sometimes hosts a plunge pool at the bottom, but it cannot be considered a reliable water source. Even when the pool is full, the water can be so silty as to be unusable.

Reach Split Level Ruin at 10.3 miles from the trailhead (2.8 miles below Todie), sitting in a giant, south-facing alcove.

Two connected structures are the centerpiece of the ruin and give Split Level its name. The rooms are stacked together on the slope, linked and staggered as in a modern split-level building. They are remarkably well preserved, with the upper one still showing its roof beams, called vigas, projecting out beyond the front wall.

Steer Clear of Walls

A kiva sits in front of the lower structure, also with a partially preserved roof with beams. Please respect the chains that protect these fragile structures and the adjacent midden as you admire the site.

Additional structures sit far above on a high ledge. These mostly appear to be more rudimentary in architectural style than the ones below, and are best viewed by stepping back from the wall and observing from a distance.

There are some excellent campsites scattered throughout the junipers and pinyons below the ruin, and some backpackers may choose to camp here on an overnight itinerary. This is an appealing option, except that water will have to be carried in at least from as far as Todie Canyon, a considerable chore.

Miles and Directions

0.0 Start at Kane Gulch Trailhead.

0.1 Pass through cattle gate.

2.1 Enter Wilderness Study Area.

4.1 Reach Junction Ruin at Grand Gulch junction.

5.1 Reach Turkey Pen Ruin.

5.5 Reach Stimper Arch viewpoint.

6.1 Bypass Fortress Canyon junction on the right (north).

7.5 Bypass Todie Canyon junction on the left (east).

9.0 Bypass large pour-off.

10.3 Reach Split Level Ruin.

Special precautions: There is generally water available at Junction Ruin and at Todie Canyon, but always ask at Kane Gulch Ranger Station for current information on trail conditions and water sources before setting out.

19 Perfect Kiva Ruin (Hike)

A beautiful canyon hike in a Grand Gulch tributary, leading to an extraordinary ruin.

Steer Clear of Walls

Start: Bullet Canyon Trailhead
Distance: 11 miles out and back
Elevation gain: 1,100 feet, mostly on return
Hiking time: 6–8 hours
Difficulty: Moderate, due to length and some route-finding
Trail surface: Dirt, sand, and rock
Best season: Spring and fall, when dry
Canine compatibility: No dogs allowed
Fees and permits: Cedar Mesa day-use permit required
MAPS: USGS topo maps: Cedar Mesa North and Pollys Pasture, Utah; **Other maps:** National Geographic Trails Illustrated #706, Grand Gulch Cedar Mesa Plateau
Trail contacts: BLM Monticello Field Office, 365 N. Main, PO Box 7, Monticello, UT 84535, (435) 587-1500, www.blm.gov/office/monticello-field -office; **Other (seasonal):** Kane Gulch Ranger Station, UT 261, 4 miles south of UT 95
Finding the trailhead: From the town of Blanding, take US 191 south for about 3 miles and turn right onto UT 95. Follow UT 95 west for 28.4 miles and turn left (south) onto UT 261. At 11 miles from UT 95, turn right (west) onto dirt San Juan CR (SJC) 251, signed for "Bullet Canyon." Follow SJC 251 for 1.1 miles to the parking area and trail register at the Bullet Canyon Trailhead.
GPS coordinates: N37° 25.84560' / W109° 56.98080'

The Hike

Bullet Canyon is the largest single tributary of Grand Gulch and one of its most popular access points. Even stripped of its archaeology, this scenic and challenging canyon makes an excellent hiking destination.

But the route down Bullet Canyon also leads to the Perfect Kiva, a unique ruin that the public is allowed to enter via the access ladder through the roof, a remarkable experience for any visitor.

Inside the Perfect Kiva.

To reach the kiva, start by signing in at the trailhead register and then head west from the parking lot. A well-worn footpath leads across the mesa top for 0.1 mile to the start of the descent route, marked by some cairns. The canyon here is wide and shallow, and a few slopes and ledges bring you to the floor.

The next 1.7 miles is like hiking in a pleasant but sometimes brushy ravine before the trail opens into a sandstone amphitheater above a series of pour-offs. Head down through the various sandstone layers, being careful to follow the cairns that mark the way. If the rock is wet it will be particularly slippery and extra caution must be used. Once through the pour-offs, you are now in a true canyon, much deeper than the section above.

At 0.4 mile past the pour-offs, watch for some cairns along the trail on the right. These cairns mark a key bypass, which takes you high on the north (right) canyon wall to avoid a boulder dam in the wash.

Follow the bypass for another 0.4 mile and then descend back to the canyon bottom. The critical junction in the wash is generally marked with more cairns to make it easier to locate on the return.

Continue to forge your way downcanyon through the brush. At 3.7 miles the South Fork of Bullet Canyon enters as a tributary from the left (southeast). In another 0.6 mile the canyon widens and flattens out at the bottom. Although the walls on either side are around 800 feet high, they are set back from the grassy meadow on the floor.

At 5.3 miles a sheer sandstone wall on the left (south) side of the canyon bends in toward the wash. Directly across from this steep wall lies the Perfect Kiva alcove, facing south into a small box canyon.

The ruin is about a third of the way up the side of the box canyon behind a few small trees at the top of a slide, and it is not easily visible from the canyon floor. You will have to do some climbing and scrambling up from the wash for the last 0.2 mile to reach the ruin ledge. The best approach is up the left side.

The centerpiece of the ruin is its namesake kiva and the square building behind it. Both have been stabilized by the BLM in order to protect them from the ravages of public visitation. Entrance to the aboveground structure is off-limits, but it is possible to descend the wooden ladder into the kiva for a one-of-a-kind experience.

Although the ladder is not the original, which was removed in the 1980s and can now be viewed at the Edge of the Cedars State Park Museum in Blanding, the replacement is a good facsimile for what the Ancestral Puebloans would have used, despite the metal bolts.

The kiva is only large enough to hold a few people at a time and lacks anywhere to sit other than the dusty floor. But with the sunlight

Perfect Kiva Ruin

streaming in from overhead, the wooden roof beams crossing the ceiling, and the earthy, smoky smell inside, the atmosphere is deeply evocative.

The kiva was originally built as a sacred space and remains so to many modern Native Americans tribes, so be sure to treat it with the appropriate care and respect.

Along with the kiva and the restored structure, there is plenty more to explore. There are several other ruins in various states of deterioration on the ledge, with a large number of metates (grinding surfaces) scattered throughout. The back of the alcove displays a pictograph gallery and also some ghost walls, which mark the locations of structures that have completely disappeared.

Leave Grinding in the Past

Don't Touch Rock Imagery or Make Your Own

The high vantage of the Perfect Kiva alcove provides an excellent view over the surrounding canyon area and usually offers plenty of shade, making the ledge an easy place to linger. If you choose to eat anything here, be sure to retreat back below the alcove, so as not to leave any rodent-attracting crumbs in the ruins.

Miles and Directions

0.0 Start at Bullet Canyon Trailhead.

0.1 Reach Bullet Canyon rim.

1.7 Reach pour-off descent.

2.1 Reach north (right) wall bypass.

2.5 End north wall bypass.

3.7 Bypass South Fork tributary junction on left (southeast).

4.3 Reach open grassy area.

5.5 Reach Perfect Kiva Ruin alcove.

11.0 End back at the trailhead.

Special precautions: When wet, not only will the access road likely be impassable, but some sections of slickrock on the trail can turn slippery and hazardous.

20 Big Man Pictograph Panel (Hike)

An ancient rock art panel with two life-size human figures in the heart of Grand Gulch.

Don't Touch Rock Imagery or Make Your Own

Start: Government Trailhead
Distance: 10.5 miles out and back
Elevation gain: 800 feet, mostly on return
Hiking time: 5–7 hours
Difficulty: Moderate to difficult, due to length, climb, and some scrambling
Trail surface: Sand, dirt, and rocks
Best season: Spring and fall, when dry
Canine compatibility: No dogs allowed
Fees and permits: Cedar Mesa day-use permit required
MAPS: USGS topo maps: Pollys Pasture, Utah; **Other maps:** National Geographic Trails Illustrated #706, Grand Gulch Cedar Mesa Plateau
Trail contacts: BLM Monticello Field Office, 365 N. Main, PO Box 7, Monticello, UT 84535, (435) 587-1500, www.blm.gov/office/monticello-field -office; **Other (seasonal):** Kane Gulch Ranger Station, UT 261, 4 miles south of UT 95
Finding the trailhead: From the town of Blanding, take US 191 south for about 3 miles and turn right onto UT 95. Follow UT 95 west for 28.4 miles and turn left (south) onto UT 261. At 13.6 miles from UT 95, turn right (west) onto San Juan CR (SJC) 245, on the opposite side of the highway from the Cigarette Springs Road. In 0.3 mile, reach a cattle guard and self-permit fee station. Continue another 2.2 miles and turn right at a junction with SJC 203 to stay on SJC 245, signed to "Government Trail." Go 3 miles and stay right again at a junction with SJC 2531 to stay on SJC 245. In another 1.9 miles, turn right at a "Government TH 1.5" sign onto a rough doubletrack. Continue on this doubletrack 1.3 miles to reach the upper parking pullout on the left, with room for a few vehicles, or 0.2 mile beyond that to where the road ends at the Government Trailhead, with room for a few more.
GPS coordinates: N37° 24.97500' / W110° 05.09400'

Big Man Pictograph Panel.

The Hike

Deep inside Grand Gulch on an exposed rock face, the Big Man Panel showcases two life-size anthropomorphic pictographs.

To get started from the trailhead, look for a worn sign reading "3 Government Trail." A nearby cattle pond shows the original purpose of the route, an old doubletrack road now fading back to its natural state. As you cross Polly Mesa, stay on the sandy path so as not to disturb the cryptobiotic soil.

Don't Bust the Crust

The mesa-top crossing ends after 2.7 miles at the rim of Grand Gulch. Directly across the canyon stands Pollys Island, a freestanding butte separated from the surrounding walls by the main fork of the canyon and an abandoned meander. It's possible to make out an inaccessible ruin beneath the island's caprock, consisting of several adjoining rooms.

Detail, Big Man Panel.

The descent begins to the right of an old metal pole that once held a sign. The trail snakes its way down the east wall of Grand Gulch for 0.6 mile, with a long traverse in the middle. Some cairns guide the way, including a large one at the bottom where you emerge onto the wash.

Memorize this key junction; you must locate it on the return to successfully find your way out.

Head upcanyon on the sandy and rocky floor, here as wide and flat as a road. After 0.2 mile a phalanx of cottonwood trees on the right guards the entrance to Pollys Canyon. Pollys hosts a number of good campsites and a spring, the only reliable water source anywhere along the route.

Continue 0.7 mile beyond the mouth of Pollys and pass around a horseshoe bend to the right. Another 0.8 mile brings you to a junction with a short, unnamed draw.

The crux of the approach lies another 0.1 mile upcanyon. Watch for where the wash takes a sharp bend to the left and a steep, sandy slope rises out of the wash on the right. This is your cue to exit the wash up the loose slope. Hopefully, other hikers will have left some footprints or a cairn to show the way.

Big Man Pictograph Panel

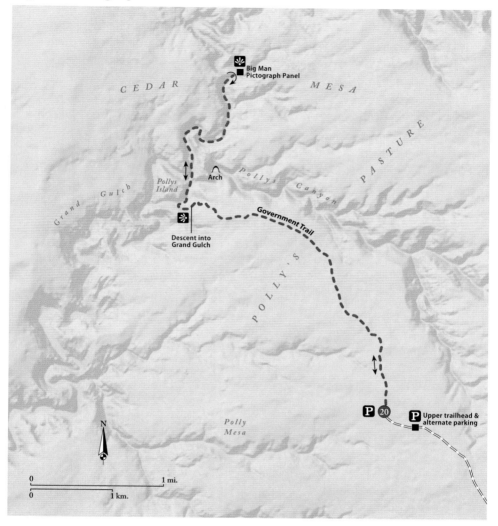

Scramble uphill through slickrock, boulders, and sandy dirt to reach a rough bench against the canyon wall. A short traverse leads you around a corner where an upcanyon view opens before you. The main attraction, however, is painted on the smooth sandstone face on your right.

The Big Man Panel is dominated by a life-size couple in red, two ancient companions together on the wall. The woman stands equal to the man in stature and significance, but he alone gives the panel its name. His anatomically correct rendering makes him easy to identify.

A constellation of other figures orbits around the central pair, including something that resembles a penguin, an animal completely alien to this desert canyon. Note that many of the white forms are actually pictographs pecked directly into the rock that were chalked by early archaeologists for easier study. The practice of chalking rock art has long since fallen out of favor—any kind of direct physical contact with the art can cause deterioration and damage—but you can take advantage of the chalk to better view the figures.

A group of boulders on the ledge below the panel provides a convenient viewing area for the art, and usually some cooling shade as well. It's easy to linger in this tranquil spot.

But eventually you will have to move on. You can retreat the way you came or follow a rough alternate route that starts on the far side of the panel and drops steeply to the wash. If you follow this alternate route, you will be able to observe how the Big Man Panel is extremely difficult to see from below, despite its size and prominent location close to the canyon rim. Once in the wash, you can head back downcanyon the way you came.

If you are feeling adventurous on the return, you can take a short (0.4 mile total) side trip into Pollys Canyon to see a natural arch. Note that many maps show the arch on the east rim of Grand Gulch just above the entrance to Pollys Canyon, which is incorrect. Head up into Pollys to see the true arch where it runs through a sandstone fin projecting from the south wall.

Miles and Directions

0.0 Start at Government Trailhead.

2.7 Reach Grand Gulch rim.

3.3 Reach Grand Gulch floor.

3.5 Bypass Pollys Canyon junction on the right (east) (0.4 mile out and back for side trip to view arch).

4.2 Pass through oxbow bend to the right (east).

5.0 Bypass unnamed canyon junction on the right (east).

5.1 Scramble route out of wash to the right (east).

5.25 Reach Big Man Panel.

10.5 End back at the trailhead.

21 Banister Ruin (Hike)

An old cowboy trail leading to a significant archaeological site in Lower Grand Gulch.

Enjoy Archaeology Without Ropes

Start: Collins Canyon (Spring) Trailhead
Distance: 10 miles out and back
Elevation gain: 600 feet, mostly on return
Hiking time: 5–7 hours
Difficulty: Moderate, due to length
Trail surface: Sand, dirt, and rocks
Best season: Spring and fall, when dry
Canine compatibility: No dogs allowed
Fees and permits: Cedar Mesa day-use permit required
MAPS: USGS topo maps: Red House Spring, Utah; **Other maps:** National Geographic Trails Illustrated #706, Grand Gulch Cedar Mesa Plateau
Trail contacts: BLM Monticello Field Office, 365 N. Main, PO Box 7, Monticello, UT 84535, (435) 587-1500, www.blm.gov/office/monticello-field -office; **Other (seasonal):** Kane Gulch Ranger Station, UT 261, 4 miles south of UT 95
Finding the trailhead: From the town of Blanding, take US 191 south for about 3 miles and turn right onto UT 95. Follow UT 95 west for 37.9 miles and turn left onto UT 276, signed for "Hanksville Via Ferry." After 6.6 miles, turn left onto San Juan CR (SJC) 260, signed for "Collins Spring Trailhead." Follow dirt road SJC 260 for 6.5 miles until it ends at the parking area. SJC 260 crosses some rough sections of slickrock but should be passable to standard 2WD vehicles when dry.
GPS coordinates: N37° 26.25120' / W110° 10.44420'

The Hike

This hike uses an old cowboy trail down Collins Canyon to reach the last significant Ancestral Puebloan ruin in Grand Gulch. Downcanyon from Banister Ruin there are almost no permanent structures; the archaeology is predominantly rock art all the way to the San Juan River.

Banister Ruin.

The trail starts from the south end of the parking lot, descending into the obvious canyon to the east. Follow cairns across sand and slickrock for 0.3 mile to reach an old wooden gate. Be sure to close the gate behind you.

In another 0.1 mile, look for a large alcove on the left (north) side of the canyon, concealed behind some van-size boulders. Duck into the alcove to discover an old cowboy camp.

A rich trove of items is scattered around the alcove, giving a glimpse into early cowboy life on Cedar Mesa. Look for a large lockbox, rusty cans, glass bottles, old pots and pans, and various other detritus of life on the range in the late 1800s. Please show the same respect to these artifacts as you would to any other archaeological resource: Look, but don't touch.

Historic Artifacts Aren't Trash

Continue downcanyon for another 0.2 mile to reach a pour-off with a bypass trail on the right. The trail appears to have been blasted directly out of the slickrock as it descends along some metal poles sticking out of the ground.

Below the pour-off the tread becomes sandier and the canyon deepens. Pass a boulder arch on the left (north) side 0.8 mile below the pour-off and then a junction with an unnamed tributary on the left around the next bend.

Continue down Collins Canyon for another 0.5 mile to reach the main channel of Grand Gulch. Be sure to study the area around this brushy flat so you will recognize the same junction on your return. Unusual rock formations on the rim are good for this purpose.

Head upcanyon (left) in Grand Gulch on the broad, flat wash. It can be slow going in the sand, but the route is generally clear and obvious. In 0.6 mile a large, saddle-shaped sandstone butte appears on the right in the middle of a rincon, an abandoned meander of the canyon. Continue past it by staying in the main channel on the left.

Over the next 0.5 mile, the walls on both sides steepen. At 1.1 miles above the rincon, wrap around a large oxbow bend to the left. This twist in the canyon bends so far back on itself that one day the main channel may breach the intervening wall to create another rincon.

Once around the bend, the trail climbs up out of the wash onto a bench to carry you through some narrow turns. Eventually you will return to the wash, and at 5 miles from the trailhead you will reach Banister Spring, which holds water at most times.

The spring is an oasis in the canyon, a thick patch of greenery in the middle of so much sand and stone. It is also the marker that you have reached the Banister Ruin. Find a gap in the brush to look up to the left (north) wall to spot the structure high on a ledge, blending in to the surrounding rock.

Banister Ruin

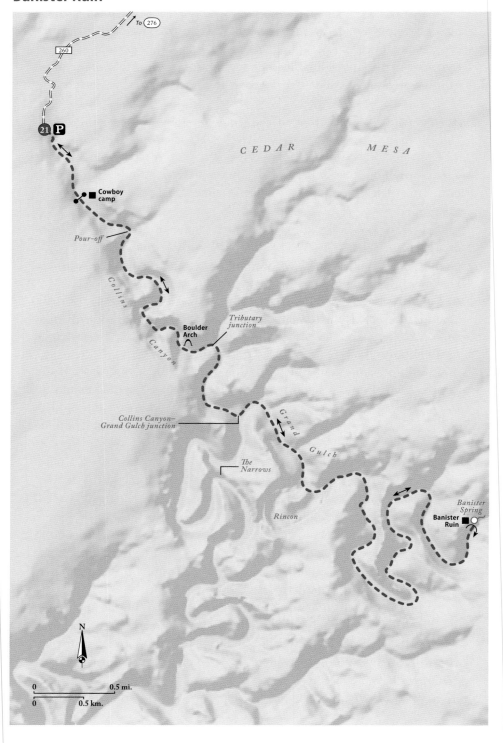

To 276

260

21 P

Cowboy camp

Pour-off

Collins Canyon

Boulder Arch

Tributary junction

Collins Canyon–
Grand Gulch junction

Grand Gulch

The Narrows

Rincon

Banister Spring

Banister Ruin

CEDAR MESA

N

0   0.5 mi.

0   0.5 km.

The name "Banister" suggests this ruin might be reached via a grand staircase, but it is a true cliff dwelling, completely inaccessible from below. Whatever method was used by the original builders to get up and down has long since disappeared, so you will have to be content to study it from the canyon floor.

The ruin derives its name from a pair of horizontal wooden beams that stretch across the front of the ledge, resembling a split-rail fence. This unusual architectural feature surely helped keep the inhabitants of the ruin safe, although it is better described as a railing than a banister.

Steer Clear of Walls

You can easily reach a well-preserved kiva on the ground beneath the main structure. Stay out of the chained-off area, which includes the ruin's midden, or trash pile. A nearby ammunition box holds a trove of information about the site and a visitor register to sign your name.

From directly below, the dizzying drop the ruin's inhabitants must have faced every day is brought into stark relief. Imagine what it must have been like climbing the canyon wall with water, food, or building materials on a regular basis. Compare these ruins with the cowboy camp you passed earlier. Although both groups must have overcome serious challenges to live and work in these canyons, the Ancestral Puebloans had a level of difficulty beyond anything the cowboys faced when they arrived 600 years later.

Miles and Directions

0.0 Start at Collins Canyon (Spring) Trailhead.

0.3 Pass through wooden gate.

0.4 Reach historical cowboy camp on left (east).

0.6 Reach pour-off bypass.

1.4 Reach boulder arch on left (north).

1.5 Bypass tributary junction on left (north).

2.0 Reach Grand Gulch junction.

2.6 Bypass rincon on right (southwest).

3.7 Pass through oxbow bend to the left (north).

5.0 Reach Banister Spring and Ruin.

10.0 End back at the trailhead.

22 Fish and Owl Canyons (Backpack)

A popular backpacking loop through a beautiful canyon complex.

Camp & Eat Away from Archaeology

Start: Fish and Owl Canyons Trailhead
Distance: 18.2-mile loop
Elevation gain: 1,600 feet
Hiking time: 2–3 days
Difficulty: Difficult, due to length, steep slopes, and route-finding. There is a hard climb out of Fish Canyon at the end, including a 12-foot crack that must be ascended to the rim.
Trail surface: Dirt, rock, and sand
Best season: Spring and fall, when dry
Canine compatibility: Dogs allowed, but not recommended
Fees and permits: Cedar Mesa backpacking permit required
MAPS: USGS topo maps: Snow Flat Spring Cave and Bluff NW, Utah; **Other maps:** National Geographic Trails Illustrated #706, Grand Gulch Cedar Mesa Plateau
Trail contacts: BLM Monticello Field Office, 365 N. Main, PO Box 7, Monticello, UT 84535, (435) 587-1500, www.blm.gov/office/monticello-field-office; **Other (seasonal):** Kane Gulch Ranger Station, UT 261, 4 miles south of UT 95
Finding the trailhead: From the town of Blanding, take US 191 south for about 3 miles and turn right onto UT 95. Follow UT 95 west for 28.4 miles and turn left (south) onto UT 261. At 5 miles from UT 95, turn left (east) onto dirt San Juan CR (SJC) 253. Follow SJC 253 for 5.2 miles to the parking area and trail register at the Fish and Owl Canyons Trailhead.
GPS coordinates: N37° 28.45980' / W109° 49.08960'

The Hike

Loop hikes are rare in the canyon country, but the route through Fish and Owl Canyons is a notable exception. Fish Creek Canyon and its tributary Owl Creek Canyon run close enough together that they are easily linked. Coupled with the spectacular rock formations that characterize these

Upper Fish Canyon.

canyons, the Fish and Owl Loop is deservedly one of the most popular backpacking routes in Bears Ears.

The loop can be completed in either direction, but the more commonly used counterclockwise direction is described here, starting down Owl Canyon and then exiting out of Fish. This allows easier route-finding in the tricky upper section of Owl, a better view of Nevills Arch, and an ascent of the 12-foot crack at the rim of Fish instead of a more difficult drop.

The trail begins on the north side of the Fish and Owl Trailhead parking lot. Turn right onto the well-worn track to the rim of Owl Canyon, 0.4 mile distant.

Follow the cairned route down through layers of sandstone. A large alcove on your right hosts several structures, including a circular kiva and some granaries. Be sure to explore the alcove, the only significant opportunity for archaeological discovery on this route. Other ruins can be seen, but only on inaccessible ledges far above the canyon floor.

Sandstone formations in Fish Canyon.

Owl Canyon spires.

Past the ruin the trail descends open slickrock through a series of pour-offs, spread over the next 2.5 miles. Some route-finding may be necessary to avoid taking the (often well-cairned) wrong path up into either of two small tributaries that enter from the west (right looking downcanyon). The descent can be tricky, especially if the rock is wet or when carrying a heavy pack, so be sure to watch your footing. The final pour-off requires a hairpin bend to the left in and out of a south-facing cul de sac to bypass successfully.

Continue 0.4 mile below the last pour-off to reach a junction with the main fork of Owl Creek Canyon. The next 2 miles offer multiple good campsites and reliable water. A popular three-day backpacking itinerary involves camping here for the first night, camping at the first water in Fish Canyon on the next night, and then exiting on the third day.

At 5.4 miles from the trailhead, Nevills Arch swings into view, capping the far left (north) end of an impressive wall of sculpted towers and hoodoos. The arch is named for Norm Nevills, a resident of the town of Mexican Hat, Utah, who is credited with the first commercial rafting operation on the San Juan River and in the Grand Canyon, starting in the 1930s. It's possible to reach the giant arch, but some route-finding and scrambling up the long talus slope is necessary.

The canyon broadens and flattens below the arch, and the track becomes drier and sandier. Despite the presence of good campsites, there is no reliable water anywhere farther down Owl Canyon.

At 7.6 miles, reach Fish Creek wash, marking the confluence of the two canyons. There are good places to camp near the confluence, and this location is a natural camping spot for a two-day itinerary. However, the nearest reliable water source is several miles up either of the two canyons, making retrieval a considerable chore.

Turn the corner and head up into Fish Canyon, a mirror image of Owl. Starting out broad and open, it eventually narrows and steepens, with many interesting sandstone formations along the walls.

Reach the first reliable water after a few miles, with minnows swimming in some of the pools. These fish have been present in the canyon at least since it was named for them around 1910, indicating the water is

Fish and Owl Canyons

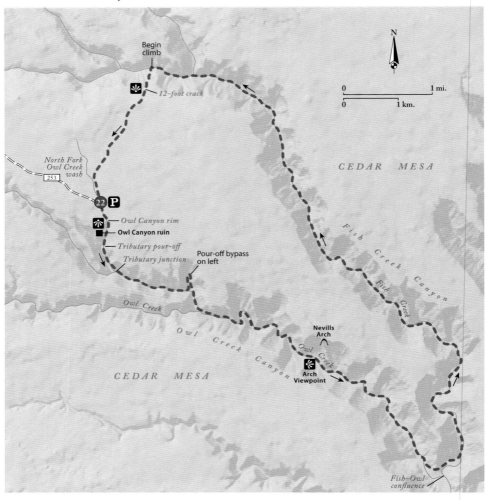

essentially permanent. The start of this water is a good location for the second night's camp on a three-day itinerary.

At 15.2 miles from the trailhead (7.6 miles above the confluence), watch for some cairns that mark the entrance of a major tributary from the left (west). Head up this tributary for another 0.7 mile to reach the challenging climb out. Just above a pour-off with some pools, more cairns and a brown BLM trail marker steer you up the south wall.

Grind up the steep slope, a gain of almost 800 feet in 0.5 mile. At the top lies the crux, a 12-foot crack that must be surmounted to reach the rim. Usually a stack of rocks provides a convenient step for assistance, but expect to use your hands to scramble up. Hauling packs with a line can help.

The last 1.8 miles of the trail run across the mesa top through pinyons and junipers to return you to the parking lot.

Miles and Directions

0.0 Start at Fish and Owl Canyons Trailhead.

0.4 Reach Owl Canyon rim.

0.5 Reach Owl Canyon ruin on right (west).

0.8 Bypass pour-off at tributary junction on right (west).

1.6 Bypass tributary junction on right (west).

2.9 Bypass pour-off on left (north).

3.3 Reach Owl Creek main channel junction.

5.4 Reach Nevills Arch viewpoint.

7.6 Reach Fish-Owl confluence.

15.2 Bypass West Fork Fish Creek junction on right (north).

15.9 Begin climb out of Fish Canyon.

16.4 Reach 12-foot crack climb at Fish Canyon rim.

17.8 Reach North Fork Owl Creek Wash.

18.2 End at Fish and Owl Canyons Trailhead.

Special Precautions

- This route contains many steep slickrock sections, especially on the descent into Owl Canyon. These sections can be tricky at the best of times and may be particularly slippery and hazardous when wet.

- There is generally water available in both Fish and Owl Canyons, but only far up either canyon, distant from the dry campsites at the sandy confluence. Ask at Kane Gulch Ranger Station for current information on water sources before setting out.

- The exit from Fish Canyon requires ascending a 12-foot crack to reach the rim. This is not technical climbing, but it does qualify as moderate scrambling. Some hikers may wish to bring a line for hauling packs. If you bring a dog (allowed, but not recommended) you may require a harness or other means of lifting him up as well.

23 Moon House Ruin (Hike)

One of the best-preserved cliff dwellings in Bears Ears, featuring a signature full-moon pictograph.

Pay Your Fees

Start: Moon House Trailhead
Distance: 1.6 miles out and back
Elevation gain: 400 feet, mostly on return
Hiking time: 1–2 hours
Difficulty: Moderate, due to short but steep and tricky trail
Trail surface: Sand, dirt, and rocks
Best season: Spring and fall, when dry
Canine compatibility: No dogs allowed
Fees and permits: Special Moon House permit required year-round
MAPS: USGS topo maps: Snow Flat Spring Cave, Utah; **Other maps:** National Geographic Trails Illustrated #706, Grand Gulch Cedar Mesa Plateau
Trail contacts: BLM Monticello Field Office, 365 N. Main, PO Box 7, Monticello, UT 84535, (435) 587-1500, www.blm.gov/office/monticello-field -office; **Other (seasonal):** Kane Gulch Ranger Station, UT 261, 4 miles south of UT 95
Finding the trailhead: From the town of Blanding, take US 191 south for about 3 miles and turn right onto UT 95. Follow UT 95 west for 28.4 miles and turn left (south) onto UT 261. In 3.9 miles, visit the Kane Gulch Ranger Station on the left to pick up your special permit. Then continue south on UT 261 for another 6.1 miles and turn left onto dirt San Juan CR (SJC) 237, signed as "Snow Flat Road." Follow SJC 237 for 8.2 miles to an unnamed road on the left with a trail register. Sign the register and continue down the dirt road for 1.3 miles to the parking area. This last road is a doubletrack with steeply banked sections and a lot of sand. If you are unsure whether your vehicle is suitable, you can park at a pullout on the right (south) side of SJC 237 by the trail register and walk the 1.3 miles to the trailhead, adding 2.6 miles to your round-trip hiking distance.
GPS coordinates: N37° 25.95300' / W109° 47.82540'

The Hike

The name "Moon House" evokes mystery and magic, two qualities with long lunar associations. There's plenty of both to be found at this ruin, one of the best-preserved ancient structures in all of Bears Ears.

Part of the traditional wonder of this site stemmed from its obscurity, tucked away in McLoyd Canyon, a minor tributary of Owl Canyon left unnamed on most maps. Canyon country explorers would stumble across the site and experience it in complete isolation. But word has gotten out about this exceptional ruin, and increasing public interest has led the BLM to implement a special permit system to limit visitor numbers and impact.

Moon House alcove.

The trail begins as a continuation of the access road at the far (north) side of the open slickrock parking area. Head out to the canyon rim and then continue left (north) until you reach a cleft in a jumble of boulders. There are multiple cairns to mark this point, the beginning of your descent.

The trail is steep and tricky, with loose footing and frequent switchbacks. Still, with no other viable route, you are surely following the same path used by the ancients centuries ago.

A pour-off halfway down requires a special bypass to negotiate. From the top of a low, overhanging ledge, you will have to drop down onto a rock-pile step. This step is not for those unsure of themselves on the trail, but if you successfully negotiate this obstacle you will have surmounted the crux of the hike.

Below the step the trail swings back along the bottom of the pour-off, following cairns as it wraps around a point. As you round the promontory through some boulders, you will catch your first glimpse of the Moon House on the opposite wall, beneath a line of hoodoos and mushroom rocks.

From this vantage you can see the full scope of the ruin, including its long outer defensive wall to the left and a number of separate rooms on the right.

After the viewpoint the trail drops steeply to the canyon floor, squeezing through some giant boulders that have tumbled from the rim. Once through the boulders, you will find yourself on exposed slickrock in the wash. There is often water in some plunge pools on the right, the same spring used by the original Moon House inhabitants in ages past.

Watch for yet more cairns leading up the canyon on the far side. The last part of the climb is a wide crack that empties out onto the slope just below the ruin.

There is usually a dedicated BLM ranger here monitoring the site. He or she can direct you on what to see and where to go, as well as answer questions about the structure. If this ranger is absent, however, you will be on your own. Be sure to exercise your utmost visit-with-respect etiquette to protect this irreplaceable resource.

Steer Clear of Walls

Moon House interior passage.

Although you should never enter any of the rooms, you can access the protected passageway behind the outer wall. Use the stacked rocks below the doorway as a step up, but be sure not to touch the walls on either side.

It's hard to see the external wall as anything but a defensive fortification. It contains multiple loop holes: gaps in the stones with sight lines to strategic points around the canyon. Some archaeologists contend that arrows could have been launched through these holes by archers safely sheltered in the passageway.

The wall has continued to serve a defensive purpose for the 700 years since the structure was abandoned, shielding the interior rooms from the elements and keeping them in an exceptional state of preservation. Mud used in wall construction has remained in place, even holding much of its original paint.

This protection has conserved the unique feature for which the ruin is named. Looking in through the doorway of one of the central rooms reveals a white stripe with down-pointing triangles painted on the interior walls. This motif is repeated in other places around the ruin, but here it uniquely possesses a circular cutout suggesting the full moon. An artificial light source is helpful to view this pictographic marvel.

Moon House Ruin

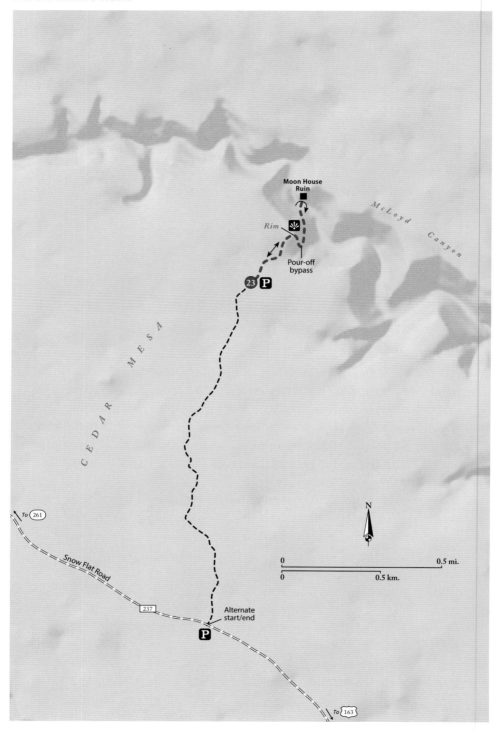

There are seven interior rooms altogether, including one hidden away down a crawl space on the far west end of the passageway. All are worthy of investigation. Note the blackened ceilings and walls, evidence of persistent use of fires for cooking and heating.

Once you are finished in the passageway, carefully exit the same way you came in. Once again, take care not to use the fragile doorframe for support.

It is worth exploring the other structures that make up the Moon House, including one with some exposed roof beams still in place. You may also find it rewarding to travel up- and downcanyon on the Moon House ledge. If the BLM ranger is on duty, he or she can provide additional guidance on where to go.

Miles and Directions

0.0 Start at Moon House Trailhead.

0.2 Reach McLoyd Canyon rim.

0.4 Reach pour-off bypass.

0.6 Reach McLoyd Wash at bottom of canyon.

0.7 Climb up north side.

0.8 Reach Moon House Ruin.

1.6 End back at the trailhead.

Special attractions: Be sure to bring some sort of artificial light source, like a headlamp, flashlight, or phone light, in order to view the ruin's namesake pictograph on a dark interior wall.

Vehicle campsites: There is no camping along the rim near the trailhead or access road. However, dispersed camping is available farther away along the Snow Flat Road and elsewhere on Cedar Mesa. Contact Kane Gulch Ranger Station for more information.

Bears Ears Buttes/ Elk Ridge Region

THE BEARS EARS BUTTES ARE THE SINGLE MOST PROMINENT FEATURE of the entire landscape, visible from miles around. Who could resist an up-close view of the landforms that lend their name to everything around them? The two destinations in this region take you to the saddle that crosses directly between the buttes and to the high country of Elk Ridge beyond. As you climb to over 8,400 feet, expect broad views over the vast canyon country. Also expect to see a different side of Bears Ears, with alpine meadows, forests of aspen and pine, and other features of a high-altitude environment, so different from the desert canyons stretched out below.

Sign at Bears Ears Pass.

24 Bears Ears Buttes (Drivable Landmark)

These buttes are the signature high points and landmarks of the entire region.

Stay on Designated Roads

Visiting time: Up to 1 hour
Best season: Spring through fall, when dry
Canine compatibility: Dogs allowed
Fees and permits: None
MAPS: USGS topo maps: Kigalia Point, Utah; **Other maps:** National Geographic Trails Illustrated #703, Manti-La Sal National Forest
Contacts: Manti-La Sal National Forest, Monticello Office, 432 E. Center St., P.O. Box 820, Monticello, UT 84535, (435) 587-2041
Finding the buttes: From the town of Blanding, take US 191 south for about 3 miles and turn right onto UT 95. Follow UT 95 west for 30.2 miles and turn right (north) onto UT 275 toward Natural Bridges National Monument. In 0.7 mile, turn right again onto good gravel San Juan CR 228. The road climbs into the Manti-La Sal National Forest and becomes FS 0088 (Elk Ridge Road). Continue on FS 0088 for 6.1 miles to Bears Ears Pass, with room for a few cars at the side of the road.
GPS coordinates: N37° 37.78020' / W109° 52.05900'

Description

At 9,000 feet, they are iconic landmarks for the region and the highest points for miles around. Of all the geologic wonders in the high desert, they were the ones chosen to lend their name to all the rest. If you're in Bears Ears country, it's hard to resist a visit to these signature buttes.

Your actual destination is Bears Ears Pass, a saddle between the buttes at 8,507 feet. On the south side is the pygmy forest of junipers, pinyons, and sage, and a view out onto the sandstone hoodoos and canyons of Cedar Mesa. To the north lies Elk Ridge and a very different view of aspens, big pines, and high alpine meadows. More than just a gap between two high points, the pass is a gateway between two ecosystems.

There is a vehicle pullout at the pass on the west (left) side of the road with space for just a few cars. A survey marker identifies the spot. There is

East Bears Ears Butte from the pass.

also a large wooden sign showing the elevation of the two buttes, which unfortunately has them mislabeled. The listed elevations are correct but reversed. The east butte is the higher one at 9,058 feet; the western butte is 8,929 feet.

If you have driven up from the south, the route described here, you may well feel a sense of relief when you step out of your car. Temperatures at the pass are often 20 degrees cooler than at Kane Gulch Ranger Station nearby on Cedar Mesa, and 30 degrees cooler than at the San Juan River, about 30 miles away and 5,000 feet below.

When seen from the pass, neither of the buttes looks anything like its signature profile; even the most imaginative viewer will have a hard time conjuring up how they resemble the ears of a bear. But up this close, their particular composition is revealed, showing their stacked sandstone cores. Mostly buried under layers of topsoil, cryptobiotic earth, and brush, look for the yellow- and red-colored rock where it is exposed on some of the slopes and high ridges.

There are some rough, unmaintained foot tracks leading into the brush and up toward the western butte. However, local Native American tribes request that people refrain from climbing the buttes out of respect for their traditional religious practices and beliefs. The buttes are sacred and not meant to be mounted without proper spiritual guidance.

You may find that the best views from the Bears Ears Buttes are not from the high point at the pass but rather all along the road during the drive back down. Seemingly around every bend, on top of every ridge,

Bears Ears Buttes, Arch Canyon Overlook #2

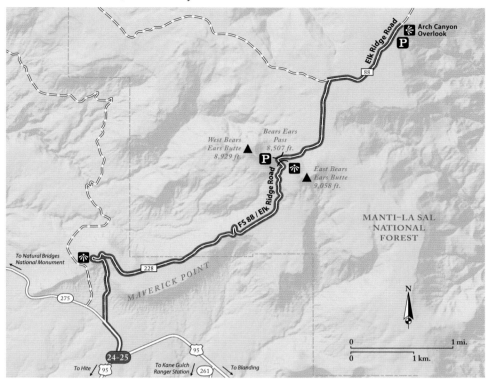

and through every gap in the trees lies a phenomenal vista out over Cedar Mesa and Natural Bridges National Monument. You will also be facing downhill, with the panoramic scene right through your windshield.

There are many convenient places to pull off and enjoy the views, take photographs, or just rest and relax. Many of these pullouts double as primitive campsites, providing a great location but no toilets, water, or other services.

Special precautions: In wet years, snow can remain on Elk Ridge into the summer and the road will be impassable until it melts out and dries.
Vehicle campsites: Multiple informal campsites lie along the road approaching Bears Ears Pass, some on land administered by the BLM and others inside the national forest boundary. There is also camping available within the national forest on Elk Ridge, both dispersed and at designated campgrounds. Contact the Manti-La Sal National Forest office for more information.

25 Arch Canyon Overlook #2 (Drivable Landmark)

A wide-ranging viewpoint in the alpine setting of Elk Ridge.

Stay on Designated Roads

[See map on page 141.]
Visiting time: Up to 1 hour
Best season: Spring through fall, if dry
Canine compatibility: Dogs allowed
Fees and permits: None
MAPS: USGS topo maps: Kigalia Point, Utah; **Other maps:** National Geographic Trails Illustrated #703, Manti-La Sal National Forest
Contacts: Manti-La Sal National Forest, Main Office, 599 W. Price River Dr., Price, UT 84501, (435) 637-2817, www.fs.usda.gov/mantilasal; **Other:** Manti-La Sal National Forest, Monticello Office, 432 E. Center St., P.O. Box 820, Monticello, UT 84535, (435) 587-2041
Finding the overlook: From the town of Blanding, take US 191 south for about 3 miles and turn right onto UT 95. Follow UT 95 west for 30.2 miles and turn right (north) onto UT 275 toward Natural Bridges National Monument. In 0.7 mile, turn right again onto good gravel San Juan CR 228. The road climbs into the Manti-La Sal National Forest and becomes FS 0088 (Elk Ridge Road). Continue on FS 0088 over Bears Ears Pass and through multiple intersections as the road switches from gravel to clay. At 9.6 miles from UT 275 (3.5 miles from Bears Ears Pass), the signed pullout for the viewpoint is on the right.
GPS coordinates: N37° 39.74400' / W109° 49.83240'

Description

This viewpoint into Arch Canyon stands less than 7 miles as the crow flies from its counterpart on Texas Flat (Arch Canyon Overlook #1). It is also about 1,600 feet higher, which makes all the difference. Despite looking into the same canyon, the two overlooks have entirely different feels.

This higher viewpoint sits on Elk Ridge, on the north side of Bears Ears Pass. This is alpine country, above 8,000 feet, and quite different from the canyons and mesas that dominate below. Snow cover is standard

Arch Canyon from the overlook.

here during the winter, sometimes lingering into May or even June in exceptional years.

If snow is present or there has been any recent precipitation, do not even think of driving here. Although the roads seem bulletproof when dry, a little added moisture can quickly transform the hard clay into a treacherous mixture of grease and glue. Even 4WD vehicles with heavy traction can be incapacitated, their tire treads gunked up and rendered useless. Worst case, you can get trapped on Elk Ridge in deteriorating weather, potentially having to wait for days before everything dries out.

But presumably you've made it to the viewpoint without incident when the roads are safe and dry. Stepping out of the car, you will notice the rich mountain scent. Where the smell of sagebrush dominates at lower elevations, the alpine forest here on Elk Ridge is predominantly a mix of aspens and ponderosa pines. If you're lucky enough to visit in the fall, you may see the forest in all its autumnal glory, as the aspens glow in a mix of golds, yellows, and reds.

Elk Ridge is the source for Arch Canyon, and this overlook stands very close to its head. Its two main tributaries, Texas Canyon and Butts Canyon, lie on either side, joining the main fork of Arch Canyon a few miles down.

Despite being one of the largest canyons on Cedar Mesa, Arch Canyon does not dominate the view; it's merely part of a broad, colorful tapestry and a welcome complement to the alpine scenery all around. What you can see of the canyon are some of the huge sandstone walls and towers that characterize this deep rift in the earth.

Beyond the canyon the view takes in a wide swath of the surrounding landscape to the east and south. Unusual for views in the Cedar Mesa region, it is possible to see all the way to the Ship Rock, a signature black monolith about 100 miles away in New Mexico.

Unfortunately, the one thing you cannot see from this viewpoint is any of the arches that give the canyon its name. For that a more intimate, close-up view is required, either from the other overlook or from the floor of the canyon itself, via the Arch Canyon Trail.

Special precautions: In wet years, snow can remain on Elk Ridge until summer and the road will be impassable until it melts out and dries.
Vehicle campsites: Multiple informal campsites lie along the road approaching Bears Ears Pass, some on land administered by the BLM and others inside the national forest boundary. There is also camping available within the national forest on Elk Ridge, both dispersed and at designated campgrounds. Contact the Manti-La Sal National Forest office for more information.

Indian Creek Region

THE INDIAN CREEK DRAINAGE DEFINES THE NORTHERN LIMITS OF BEARS Ears, centerpiece of a narrow arm of land that reaches from the town of Monticello and the north slopes of the Abajo (Blue) Mountains to the periphery of Canyonlands National Park. Along the way, expect some of the same stunning canyon-country scenery found farther south—with the additional bonus of the otherworldly rock formations of The Needles District, an ancient erosional playground of the Colorado River. An easy drive can also take you to Newspaper Rock, one of the finest petroglyph panels anywhere in the desert Southwest.

Colorado River and red-rock layers north of Needles Overlook.

26 Harts Draw Road (Scenic Drive)

An easy, paved drive on the north side of the Abajo Mountains with wide-ranging views of high mountains and desert canyons.

Stay on Designated Roads

Starting point: Where Shay Mountain Road branches off FS 101 just past the Shay Mountain Lookout, west of Monticello in the Abajo Mountains.
GPS coordinates: N37° 54.43560' / W109° 29.57160'
Finding the start: From the intersection of US 191 and US 491 in the town of Monticello, take Main Street/US 191 south. In 0.2 mile, turn right onto West 200 South. In 0.4 mile, bear left onto Abajo Road, which soon leaves town and becomes FS 101 (also San Juan CR 101 or North Creek Road). Continue on FS 101 for 9.6 miles, past multiple campgrounds and side roads, to reach the Shay Mountain Lookout. Go past the lookout for another 0.6 mile to a junction with Shay Mountain Road (also Shay Trail Ridge) on the left. Stay right on FS 101, which becomes Harts Draw Road (labeled on some maps as FS 136).
Total distance: 8.5 miles

Key Points

0.0 Start at junction with Shay Mountain Road.

2.0 Sweeping left turn with view into Canyonlands National Park.

4.0 Pullout on the right with Shay Mountain view.

4.3 Switchback to the right.

5.6 Exit Manti-La Sal National Forest.

8.5 End at junction with UT 211 (Indian Creek Scenic Byway).

Time required: Up to 1 hour
Best season: Any time when not blocked by snow; impressive colors in the fall
MAPS: USGS topo maps: Shay Mountain and Monticello Lake, Utah; **Other maps:** National Geographic Trails Illustrated #703, Manti-La Sal National Forest

Contacts: Manti-La Sal National Forest, Monticello Office, 432 E. Center St., P.O. Box 820, Monticello, UT 84535, (435) 587-2041

Fees and permits: None

Minimum vehicle requirements: Any standard passenger vehicle can complete the drive.

Difficulty: Easy

Road conditions: Paved for its entire length

Vehicle campsites: There are multiple Forest Service campgrounds along FS 101.

The Drive

The Abajo Mountains, also known as the Blue Mountains, rise above the towns of Blanding and Monticello. Visible from much of the Bears Ears region, the Abajos reach to over 11,000 feet and are landmarks that have held significance for local people for thousands of years.

Like the La Sal Mountains near Moab farther north, the Abajos were formed some 25 million years ago when magma bubbled up from deep in the earth, forcing the sandstone on the surface toward the sky. Most of the sedimentary sandstone eroded away, exposing the harder igneous rock that forms the core of the mountains visible today.

Harts Draw Road view toward Canyonlands National Park.

Harts Draw Road

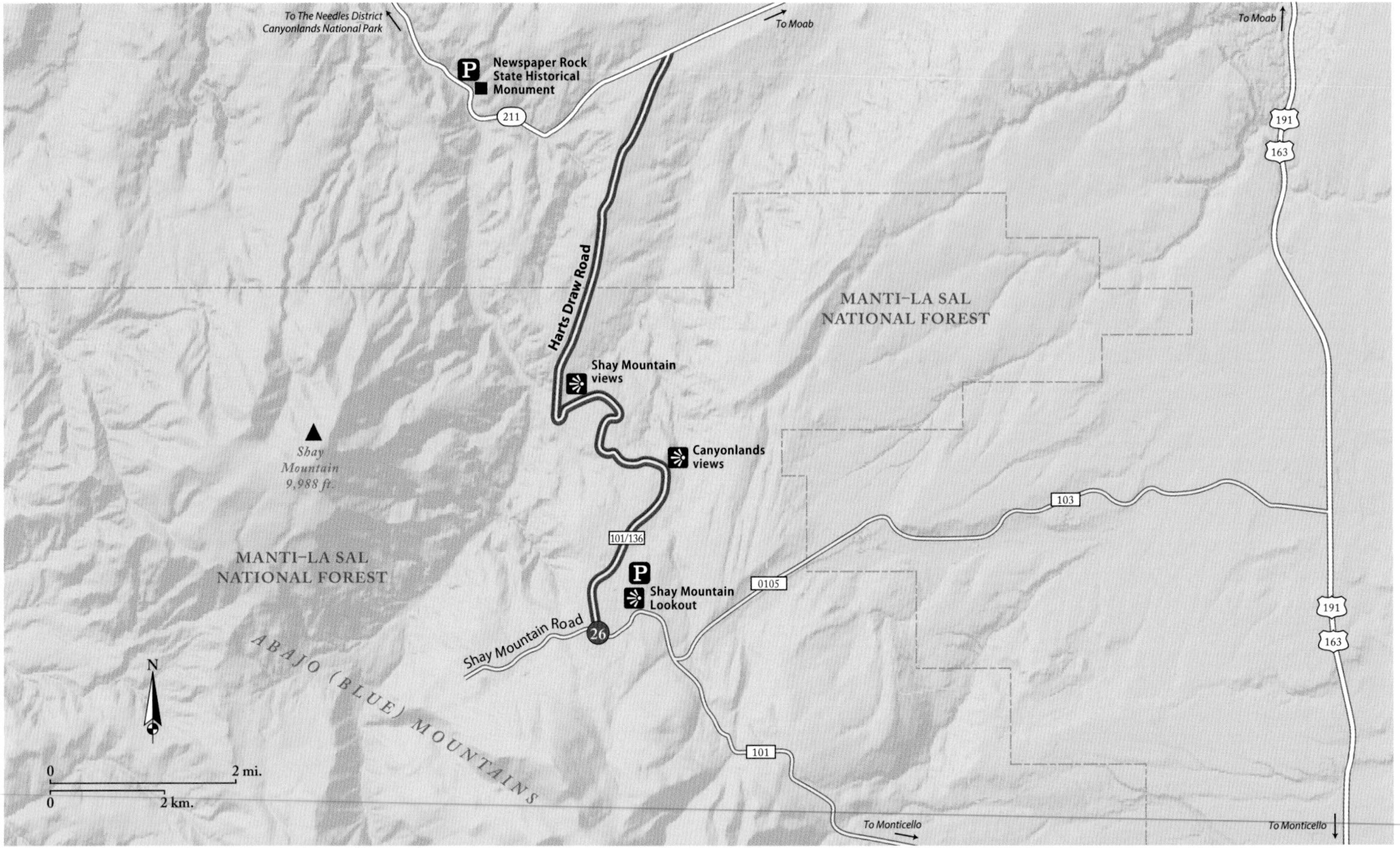

To Moab

To Moab

191 163

191 163

To Monticello

To Monticello

MANTI-LA SAL
NATIONAL FOREST

103

0105

101

Newspaper Rock
State Historical
Monument

211

To The Needles District
Canyonlands National Park

Harts Draw Road

Shay Mountain
views

Canyonlands
views

101/136

Shay Mountain
Lookout

26

Shay Mountain Road

Shay
Mountain
9,988 ft.

MANTI-LA SAL
NATIONAL FOREST

ABAJO (BLUE) MOUNTAINS

N

2 mi.

2 km.

0

0

Harts Draw Road runs along the northern flank of the Abajos, linking their high alpine slopes with the lower-elevation canyon country beyond. The route is at its most dramatic during the autumn, when the highlands are alive with fall colors, but it has plenty to offer year-round.

The road can be driven in either direction but is described here traveling north, which allows you to face all of the best views as you go.

Although Harts Draw Road technically does not start until more than 10 miles out of Monticello, the scenic views begin right as you leave town. The approach road climbs up into the mountains, leaving the desert behind for forested slopes and peaks. Multiple campgrounds branch off the main road, popular with locals and visitors alike.

The Shay Mountain Lookout appears just before the drive officially begins, on the west side of a saddle that crosses over the road's highest point at 8,432 feet. Past the lookout it's all downhill.

Once you are on Harts Draw Road, the views open in front of you. The La Sal Mountains rise sharply to the north, more than 1,000 feet higher than the Abajos and topping out at the summit of Mount Tukuhnikivatz at 12,489 feet.

Shay Mountain lies immediately to the west at 9,988 feet. Its east flank, facing the road, shows the geologic forces that created these mountains eons ago. The lower slopes are characterized by the eroded sandstone that connects it with the landscape to the north.

The open space to the northwest provides a vast panorama of sculpted desert canyons. On a clear day it's possible to see much of Canyonlands National Park, including the high mesas of the Island in the Sky District across the Colorado River, some 40 miles distant. In between, much of The Needles District is spread out before you.

The vast jumble of mesas, towers, and canyons makes it hard to identify specific landmarks, but the two pointy Sixshooter Peaks (North, 6,374 feet; and South, 6,132 feet) stand out, even at this distance. The peaks stand close to The Needles District's main entrance and are named for their resemblance to pistols aimed at the sky.

As you follow the twists and turns down the road, your vantage will shift accordingly. A few pullouts along the way allow you to stop and take pictures or just enjoy the view. The road then straightens out for the last few miles before ending at a T junction with UT 211. This highway is the access road into The Needles and the Indian Creek area, home to the Newspaper Rock Petroglyph Panel just a few miles away.

27 Newspaper Rock Petroglyph Panel (Drivable Landmark)

A famous rock art panel along the highway to Canyonlands National Park.

Don't Touch Rock Imagery or Make Your Own

Visiting time: Up to 1 hour
Best season: Year-round
Canine compatibility: Leashed dogs allowed
Fees and permits: None
MAPS: USGS topo maps: Shay Mountain, Utah; **Other maps:** National Geographic Trails Illustrated #703, Manti-La Sal National Forest
Contacts: BLM Monticello Field Office, 365 N. Main, PO Box 7, Monticello, UT 84535, (435) 587-1500, www.blm.gov/office/monticello-field-office
Finding the trailhead: From the intersection of US 191 and US 491 in the town of Monticello, take US 191 north for 14.3 miles and turn left (west) onto UT 211 toward The Needles District of Canyonlands National Park. Follow UT 211 for 12.3 miles to the parking area for Newspaper Rock on the right.
GPS coordinates: N37° 59.29440' / W109° 31.08960'

The Panel

Newspaper Rock is one of the best-known rock art sites anywhere in Utah—and the entire Southwest. An exposed sandstone face provides a natural canvas of black desert varnish that artists have exploited for centuries.

The rock sits along UT 211 on the east wall of Indian Creek Canyon, just 22 miles short of the entrance to The Needles District of Canyonlands National Park. The Indian Creek corridor provides the only easy access into The Needles region.

The importance of this route has remained unchanged for thousands of years. For anyone wishing to descend from the high desert around the Abajo Mountains to the canyons of the Colorado River, this is the way to go.

The direct placement of Newspaper Rock on this route is surely no accident; it is right along a main travel artery, openly displayed to anyone passing by. Given the heavy use of animal imagery on the petroglyphs, it's likely this passage was a frequently used wildlife corridor as well.

Newspaper Rock.

The images, figures, and shapes on the rock are all petroglyphs, pecked, carved, or etched directly into the stone. The contrast between the dark overcoat and the sand-colored layer beneath is particularly high here, providing unusually sharp edges and definition to the images.

The oldest carvings are thought to be about 1,500 years old. These, however, are not the most vivid of the art forms but are instead obscured underneath. If you look carefully in some spots, it is possible to make out other, fainter images behind the primary figures. These fainter ones have been "written over," a process known as superimposition.

The newest images on Newspaper Rock are from the early twentieth century, the dawning of the modern era in the Southwest. Symbols like a wagon wheel, a man shooting an arrow from horseback, and some figures that appear to be wearing chaps and spurs reveal their roots in the cowboy age.

The art thus spans three different time periods as recognized by modern archaeologists: prehistoric, historic, and protohistoric. The difference between prehistoric and historic eras in a particular culture is the

Newspaper Rock petroglyphs.

existence of a written record. Protohistoric refers to a period in between, during which a culture has not yet developed writing but other cultures have written about it. The key dividing line in the Southwest is the arrival of the first Europeans, who brought their writing with them.

Many symbols possess recognizable shapes and subjects. Some four- and six-toed footprints walk up the wall, adjacent to a series of hoofprints

Newspaper Rock Petroglyph Panel

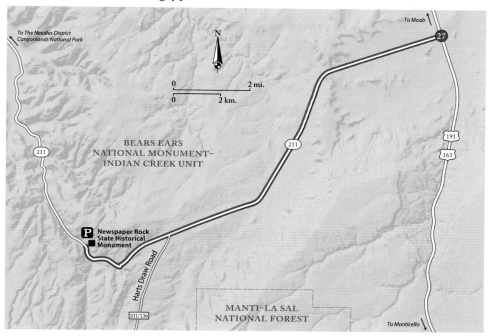

and the horned ungulate that must have produced them. Lots of similar elk, deer, and bison are visible, popular game for hunters both modern and ancient. Paw prints, however, seem to have no obvious source, since the animals that would have made them are generally absent.

Even though so many of the figures are identifiable to the modern viewer, their larger meanings and narratives have been lost. Perhaps this makes Newspaper Rock poorly named. The news is typically "of the day," the fresher and more immediate the better. The ancient symbols here have been hailing passersby for centuries, transcending the moments of their creation. Newspaper Rock is really more of a timeless billboard or signpost. **Vehicle campsites:** There is no immediate camping in this area, but there is camping available at Canyonlands National Park at the end of UT 211, in the Canyon Rims Recreation Area to the north on US 191, and to the south in the Manti-La Sal National Forest. Contact the associated management agencies for more information.

Don't Build Fire Rings

28 Needles Overlook (Drivable Landmark)

A panoramic viewpoint over a wild landscape of eroded rock.

Stay on Designated Roads

Visiting time: 1–2 hours
Best season: Year-round, when road is clear
Canine compatibility: Dogs allowed
Fees and permits: None
MAPS: USGS topo maps: Lockhart Basin, Utah; **Other maps:** National Geographic Trails Illustrated #210, Canyonlands National Park; and #501, Moab South
Contacts: BLM Moab Field Office, 82 E. Dogwood, Moab, UT 84532, (435) 259-2100, www.blm.gov/office/moab-field-office
Finding the overlook: From the intersection of US 191 and US 491 in the town of Monticello, take US 191 north for 21.2 miles and turn left onto Needles Overlook Road (San Juan CR 133) into the Canyon Rims Recreation Area. Follow paved Needles Overlook Road for 15 miles and then stay left at an intersection with Hatch Point Road to stay on Needles Overlook Road. Continue another 6.9 miles to where the road ends at the overlook.
GPS coordinates: N38° 15.59700' / W109° 41.77080'

Description

In the area north of the Abajo Mountains and south of Moab, Canyonlands National Park gets all the attention. That leaves other worthy destinations underused, including this gem of an overlook in the Canyon Rims Recreation Area. The long drive, although paved the entire way, may also be a deterrent to some potential visitors. Their loss can be your gain.

From the parking area a short, paved loop circles through the nearby sandstone outcroppings to connect with multiple dirt paths that lead to the rim. Various picnic tables lie scattered throughout the rocks, pleasant places to spend some time. With a little luck you might find one in the shade.

Views abound on all sides, with developed overlooks in several locations around the point. The largest one is at the end of the promontory,

Picnic area at Needles Overlook.

Shaded viewpoint at Needles Overlook.

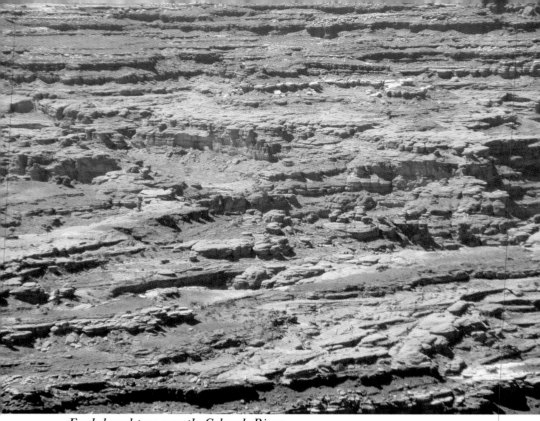

Eroded sandstone near the Colorado River.

complete with sunshade, bench, and display kiosk to let you know what you are looking at.

There are also toilets, trash bins, and other amenities offered, although Needles Overlook is for day use only; there is no water available and no camping is allowed.

The overlook stands on the east rim of a great rift in the earth, a temple of erosion with the Colorado River at its center. However, unlike the Grand Canyon with its cavernous depths and sheer drops, the landscape here is shallower, the rock layers carved into a million different shapes and textures.

True to its name, the overlook provides a grand overview of The Needles District of Canyonlands National Park, just to the southwest. The high-elevation vantage at 6,295 feet allows you to take in the entire sweep of the landscape in a way that is not possible from within the park itself; the Needles Visitor Center is more than 1,300 feet below. Look for the district's signature spires lined up on a prominent ridge, running down toward the Colorado.

Needles Overlook

The Needles is not the only visible section of Canyonlands. Look for the labyrinthine sandstone confines of The Maze, one of the most remote and challenging landscapes anywhere in the United States, directly across the canyon to the west. Island in the Sky sits high on the opposite rim north of The Maze, at a similar elevation to where you stand. Its well-known White Rim formation appears as a light stripe running along the edge of a broad bench above the Colorado's inner canyon.

Gazing down at the fantastic landscape in all its glory, it's hard to imagine how the force of water alone could have created such a wide range of shapes and forms. Yet as unlikely as it seems, everything you see is a testament to the relentless power of the wild Colorado and its tributaries, compounded through millions of years.

Unfortunately, although evidence of the river's action is everywhere, the river itself is largely hidden. That includes an unusual feature known as The Loop, a double horseshoe bend only about 7 miles away. Also concealed is the Green River junction, one of the most important confluences on the Colorado's entire length and the point where all three of Canyonlands' sections meet.

Not surprisingly for this harsh desert landscape, there is little evidence of human activity. People have been active in this land for centuries, long before the arrival of the first European settlers, but there is little permanent record of their passage. Other than the limited development at the overlook itself, the most obvious human impact is the Lockhart Basin Road, a dirt track running along the bench about 1,500 feet directly below. Beyond that, there is nothing but the vast canyon-country wilderness.

Vehicle campsites: The BLM provides multiple developed campgrounds in the Canyon Rims Recreation Area, including Windwhistle Campground on the Needles Overlook Road and Hatch Point Campground nearby. Reservations are generally not required unless you are part of a large group. Contact the BLM office in Moab for more information.

Don't Build Fire Rings

Natural Bridges National Monument

More than one hundred years before there was a Bears Ears, Natural Bridges was the signature national monument for this part of Utah. Established by President Theodore Roosevelt in 1908, the monument sought to preserve three landmark natural bridges, geological rarities despite their resemblance to the sandstone arches that regularly occur throughout the surrounding canyons. Sitting on the northern end of Cedar Mesa and straddling several tributaries of the massive White Canyon system, Natural Bridges National Monument has always been worth a visit all on its own. Although its deep canyons and cultural riches are similar to other places on Cedar Mesa, its namesake natural bridges can be found nowhere else. Plus, extensive park development, including campgrounds, a visitor center, and other amenities, make this a welcoming destination for travelers.

Massive Kachina Bridge.

29 Natural Bridges Loop Drive (Scenic Drive)

An easy drive to Natural Bridges National Monument's three signature spans.

Pay Your Fees

Starting point: Natural Bridges National Monument Park Headquarters and Visitor Center, on UT 275.
GPS coordinates: N37° 36.54180' / W109° 58.61700'
Finding the start: From the town of Blanding, take US 191 south for about 3 miles and turn right onto UT 95. Follow UT 95 west for 30.2 miles and turn right (north) onto UT 275 toward Natural Bridges National Monument. Follow UT 275 for 4.5 miles to the visitor center on the right.
Total distance: 9.7 miles

Key Points

0.0 Start at visitor center.

0.5 Reach UT 275/Bridge View Drive loop road junction.

1.9 Reach Sipapu Bridge Overlook.

2.5 Reach Sipapu Bridge Trailhead.

2.9 Reach Horse Collar Ruin Overlook.

4.8 Reach Kachina Bridge Overlook and Trailhead.

6.7 Reach Owachomo Bridge Overlook and Trailhead.

9.2 Return to UT 275/Bridge View Drive loop road junction.

9.7 End at visitor center.

Time required: 2–5 hours, depending on time spent at overlooks
Best season: Year-round
Canine compatibility: Leashed dogs allowed outside vehicles, but no dogs allowed on hiking trails
MAPS: USGS topo maps: Kane Gulch and Moss Back Butte, Utah; **Other maps:** National Geographic Trails Illustrated #703, Manti-La Sal National Forest
Contacts: Natural Bridges National Monument, HC 60, Box 1, Lake Powell, UT 84533-0001, (435) 692-1234, www.nps.gov/nabr

Fees and permits: Park entrance fee required

Minimum vehicle requirements: Any standard passenger vehicle can complete the drive.

Difficulty: Easy

Road conditions: Paved for its entire length

Vehicle campsites: There is a first-come, first-served campground in the park near the visitor center. The campground is open year-round and requires an additional fee on top of the park entrance fee.

The Drive

Arches are common in the canyon country, but natural bridges are few and far between. Any number of erosive processes can create an arch, but a bridge must span a creek bed and can only be created by the action of flowing water.

Three of these rare formations sit on the northern edge of Cedar Mesa, protected by President Theodore Roosevelt's creation of Natural Bridges National Monument in 1908.

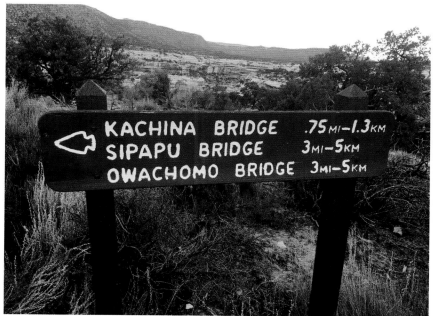

Signage along the loop drive.

Natural Bridges Loop Drive

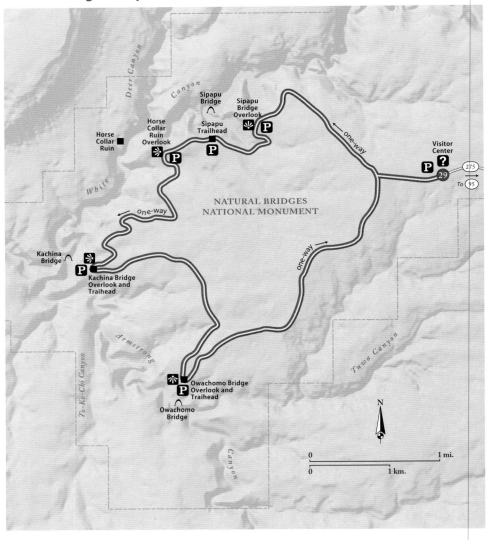

The three bridges span White Canyon and its tributaries, part of a large canyon system that drains the west side of Elk Ridge and runs to the Colorado River. All three can be easily viewed via the park's one-way loop road, starting at the end of UT 275 just past the visitor center.

Each bridge has an overlook and a trailhead right off the road. The overlooks provide viewing platforms and information on the bridges' geology. The trailheads are the various access points for the loop trail that runs along the canyon bottom, linking all three bridges. Other services are available along the drive as well, such as trash cans, restrooms, and a picnic area.

First up is Sipapu Bridge, with the greatest span of the three at 268 feet and the greatest height at 220 feet. *Sipapu* is a Hopi word meaning "place of emergence," after the mythical gateway the Hopi believe their ancestors passed through to enter this world. The same word is used for the small hole generally found in the floor of a kiva, adjacent to the fire pit and opposite the air intake.

Despite its size, Sipapu Bridge can be difficult to spot from the overlook because of how well it blends into its surroundings. Often the best way to see it is to look for the shadow it projects underneath.

Just past Sipapu is the Horse Collar Ruin Overlook. There is no natural bridge here but instead an Ancestral Puebloan archaeological site in an alcove on the floor of White Canyon. The extensive ruin displays a piece of the rich cultural heritage of this area and is more easily viewed from the rim than from the canyon floor itself.

Next is Kachina Bridge, 210 feet high and spanning 204 feet. It is most notable for the thickness of its roof, 93 feet from top to bottom, almost double that of Sipapu and more than 10 times that of spindly Owachomo. All natural bridges wear thin and eventually collapse in their old age; Kachina is the youngest and sturdiest bridge in the monument and still has a long way to go.

Although not visible from the rim, Kachina's abutments and surrounding walls are covered in ancient rock art. The bridge lies at the confluence of Armstrong Canyon and White Canyon, and the art may have served to mark this important junction for long-ago travelers. The bridge derives its name from some of this art, which resembles symbols often drawn onto ceremonial kachina dolls.

Last up is Owachomo Bridge, the smallest of the three at 106 feet high and 180 feet across. It is also the oldest, indicated by the thinness of its roof. Unusually, Owachomo no longer spans any creek and was apparently formed by the combined action of two separate water courses beneath it. The name is from a Hopi word meaning "rock mound," for a conspicuous sandstone dome above the bridge's east side.

Past Owachomo, the road returns to the beginning of the loop and then back out to the visitor center where you began.

30 Natural Bridges Loop Hike (Hike)

The best way to explore the cultural heritage and unique rock formations of Natural Bridges National Monument.

Don't Bust the Crust

Start: Sipapu Bridge Trailhead
Distance: 8.8-mile loop
Elevation gain: 800 feet
Hiking time: 5–8 hours
Difficulty: Moderate to difficult, due to length, some route-finding, and some steep ladder descents
Trail surface: Sand, dirt, and rocks
Best season: Year-round
Canine compatibility: No dogs allowed
Fees and permits: Park entrance fee required
MAPS: USGS topo maps: Kane Gulch and Moss Back Butte, Utah; **Other maps:** National Geographic Trails Illustrated #703, Manti-La Sal National Forest
Trail contacts: Natural Bridges National Monument, HC 60, Box 1, Lake Powell, UT 84533, (435) 692-1234, www.nps.gov/nabr
Finding the trailhead: From the town of Blanding, take US 191 south for about 3 miles and turn right onto UT 95. Follow UT 95 west for 30.2 miles and turn right (north) onto UT 275 toward Natural Bridges National Monument. Follow UT 275 for 4.5 miles to the visitor center on the right to pay the park fee. From the visitor center, drive the park loop road (Bridge View Drive) 2.5 miles to the Sipapu Bridge Trailhead.
GPS coordinates: N37° 36.79980' / W110° 00.55140'

The Hike

This loop hike links all three of the monument's signature natural bridges: Sipapu, Kachina, and Owachomo. Since the route is a loop, it's possible to start anywhere and travel in either direction, but the description here begins at Sipapu Bridge and travels counterclockwise, same as the park road.

Owachomo Bridge from Armstrong Canyon.

From the Sipapu Bridge Trailhead, the path carves a steep descent into White Canyon. It's easy to see where the canyon gets its name; the Cedar Mesa Sandstone here is creamy white, not the darker yellow commonly found elsewhere.

A metal staircase helps you down an early cliff band. A rare grove of Douglas firs and ponderosa pines grows along the wall below, trees usually restricted to higher elevations or wetter climates. Several wooden ladders drop down the sheer sandstone, including two right before you reach the bottom. These ladders are sturdy and well anchored, but the downclimbs may be difficult for those afraid of heights.

Below the ladders, emerge into the brush on the canyon floor at the foot of Sipapu Bridge, soaring 220 feet overhead. The true scale of the bridge becomes evident when you stand underneath.

Head downcanyon from Sipapu along the wash, keeping an eye out for archaeology along the way. The White Canyon system was traveled and occupied for centuries by the Ancestral Puebloans, who left ample traces of their passing.

Deer Canyon enters from the north (right looking downcanyon) at 1.4 miles, and then the Horse Collar Ruin alcove appears on the same side in another 0.2 mile. The alcove is on a bench well above the wash and is easy to miss by walking underneath.

Reaching the ruin requires a challenging slickrock scramble, so most hikers are advised to study the ruin from a distance. The best vantage is actually from the overlook on the rim, a stop on the park loop road. The ruin itself is named for one of its structures, a two-room "duplex" with unusual doorframes that resemble horse collars—or toilet seats, for those less familiar with equestrian gear.

Steer Clear of Walls

Continue downcanyon to reach the bulky span of Kachina Bridge at 3.1 miles. Although similar in height to Sipapu at 210 feet, its thick roof makes the opening underneath much smaller. Be sure to explore the walls all around the base of Kachina, where rock art abounds. Look for both pictographs and petroglyphs on the sandstone, some bright and vivid and others more faded and subtle.

Owachomo Bridge.

Sipapu Bridge from White Canyon.

Don't Touch Rock Imagery or Make Your Own

The trail makes an important turn under the bridge, leaving White Canyon and heading up Armstrong Canyon on the left. In 0.1 mile look for the exit trail to the Kachina Overlook. Follow this route up and out

Natural Bridges Loop Hike

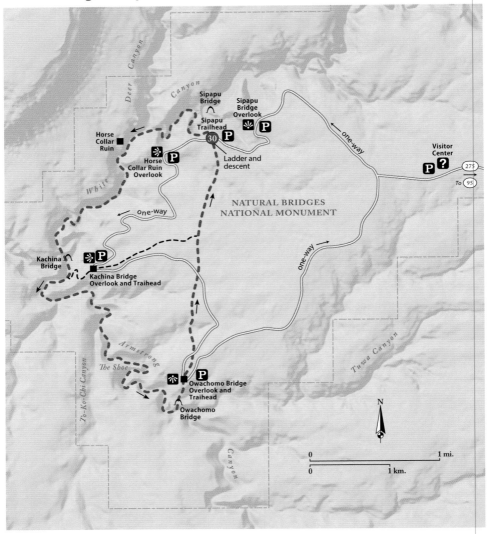

of the wash until you reach a junction partway up the slope. Take the side trail and follow it around the head of a pour-off.

Continue upcanyon in Armstrong, which is shallower than the section of White Canyon you hiked down before. Stay in the main channel, bypassing some minor tributaries on either side, including To-ko-chi Canyon, which enters through a narrow gap in the wall at 4.6 miles.

Wrap around a distinctive sandstone horn known as "The Shoe" at 5.3

miles, and then watch for where the route climbs up on the left to avoid a boulder dam in the wash.

Stay high on a ledge for another 1.1 miles to reach the elegant span of Owachomo Bridge, 106 feet high, on the left (north) wall. Unlike the first two bridges, Owachomo does not span the canyon you are hiking in. You will need to cross underneath it and exit Armstrong Canyon to reach the trailhead and overlook.

The climb to the Owachomo Trailhead is the easiest of all the bridge access routes, requiring no ladders. Once at the trailhead, cross the park road and follow the trail over the mesa top for 2.1 miles to return to Sipapu. The mesa trail provides no canyon or bridge views, but offers a pleasant walk through the pygmy forest of junipers and pinyon pines. Be sure to avoid stepping on the abundant cryptobiotic soil along the way.

Miles and Directions

0.0 Start at Sipapu Bridge Trailhead.

0.6 Ladder descent.

0.7 Reach Sipapu Bridge.

1.4 Bypass Deer Canyon junction on right (north).

1.6 Reach Horse Collar Ruin.

3.1 Reach Kachina Bridge/Armstrong Canyon junction.

3.2 Reach Kachina Bridge Trail/Armstrong Canyon pour-off bypass.

4.6 Bypass To-ko-chi Canyon junction on right (south).

5.3 Pass The Shoe rock formation.

6.4 Reach Owachomo Bridge/Tuwa Canyon junction.

6.7 Reach Owachomo Bridge Overlook and Trailhead.

6.9 Cross park loop road.

7.8 Cross park loop road.

7.9 Reach Kachina Bridge Trail junction.

8.8 End at Sipapu Bridge Trailhead.

Vehicle campsites: There is a first-come, first-served campground in the park near the visitor center. The campground is open year-round and requires an additional fee on top of the park entrance fee.

Dark Canyon Region

Known informally as the "Grand Canyon of Utah," mighty Dark Canyon drains the high alpine terrain of Elk Ridge, emptying into the Colorado River near the old settlement of Hite. Deep enough to penetrate the ancient layers of bedrock that underlie much of the canyon country, the bottom of Dark Canyon reveals a slice of geologic history visible few other places in Bears Ears. The challenging but rewarding Sundance Trail can take you all the way down. An easier trip in this region can be made to the archaeologically unusual Fry Canyon Ruin, a structure built in a chasm much narrower than was typically used by the Ancestral Puebloans.

Dark Canyon from the Sundance Trail.

31 Fry Canyon Ruin (Drivable Landmark)

An easy-to-reach viewpoint to a rare slot-canyon ruin.

Stay on Designated Roads

Visiting time: Up to 1 hour
Best season: Year-round, when dry
Canine compatibility: Dogs allowed
Fees and permits: None
MAPS: USGS topo maps: Jacobs Chair, Utah; **Other maps:** National
Geographic Trails Illustrated #703, Manti-La Sal National Forest
Contacts: BLM Monticello Field Office, 365 N. Main, PO Box 7, Monticello, UT
84535, (435) 587-1500, www.blm.gov/office/monticello-field-office
Finding the trailhead: From the town of Blanding, take US 191 south for
about 3 miles and turn right onto UT 95. Follow UT 95 west for 49.8 miles
to the settlement of Fry Canyon. Continue past the settlement on UT 95 for
another 1.1 miles and turn right at milepost 70.4 onto dirt San Juan CR (SJC)
2141. Follow SJC 2141 for another 0.6 mile to where it ends at the slickrock
overlook. SJC 2141 is generally passable to standard 2WD vehicles when dry.
GPS coordinates: N37° 38.98020' / W110° 09.54240'

The Ruin

There are two ruins at Fry Canyon, one ancient and one modern. The first
is an Ancestral Puebloan archaeological site and the second is a ghost
town, and they both show the difficulties of living in this harsh desert
landscape.

Fry Canyon is named for Charlie Fry, a hermit prospector who lived
off a spring at the head of the canyon in the 1890s. This lonely outpost
saw few visitors beyond the occasional cattle rancher until the 1950s,
when a brief uranium boom led to a small flurry of development. The
tiny town built a post office and the Fry Canyon Lodge hosted regular
visitors, but the uranium boom died in the 1960s with the passing of the
Atomic Age.

The old lodge is the large building just off the highway, now shuttered
for many years. Fry Spring is on private property with no public access,

Upper Fry Canyon.

and some of the water has been contaminated by tailings from the abandoned mining operation.

Still in occasional use, however, is an airstrip through the pinyon and juniper forest. The road to the ruin actually runs right across it, although

Fry Canyon Ruin

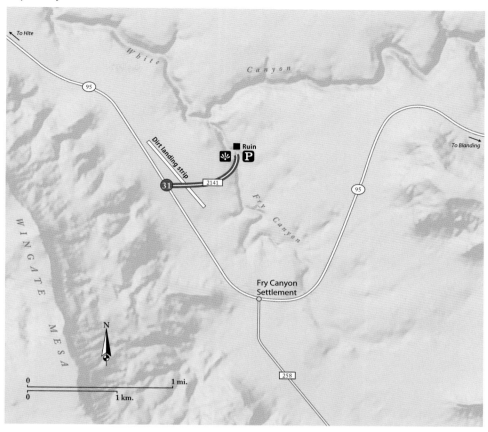

most visitors fail to recognize the clearing as anything more than a meadow. It's hard to picture too many planes landing in the grass and brush, but the orange windsock on the southwest side gives it away.

On the far side of the airstrip, the short dirt road ends at a slickrock clearing on Fry Canyon's southern rim. The ruin lies directly across the canyon beneath a bend in the sandstone wall, with several rooms in varied states of decay. Some of the structures deeper in the alcove have been better protected from the elements, with distinct doors still visible, while the ones in front have not fared as well.

All the rooms are built in a similar style, with flat stones stacked together to form walls. No mortar is used and the building corners are rough and uneven. This crude building style probably dates the ruin to

Fry Canyon Ruin alcove.

the Pueblo I period (750–900 CE), before more advanced architectural styles appeared.

Fry Canyon is neither particularly wide nor deep at the overlook, but there is no easy way across. Sheer sandstone walls prevent even reaching the canyon floor. Looking to the southeast (right) you can see where the inner canyon narrows to a corkscrew slot, tight enough that it's questionable whether anyone could squeeze through.

This highlights a big difference between the bulk of the canyons here, which drain directly into the Colorado River, and those on Cedar Mesa, which flow into the San Juan. The Cedar Mesa canyons are wide with dirt benches and are easily passable in large sections, making them suitable for settlement and agricultural development. The high density of archaeological sites and rich cultural heritage evident in Grand Gulch and its tributaries today are the result.

In contrast, Fry Canyon features frequent narrow slots and impassable drops. Descending on foot is a challenge, a canyoneering adventure requiring use of ropes and the occasional swim. Despite the abundant water, there is little or no soil for growing crops, and sunlight is often unable to penetrate the canyon depths.

This makes Fry Canyon unfavorable to human travel, agriculture, and habitation. Archaeological sites like Fry Canyon Ruin are thus comparatively rare, and should be appreciated all the more.

Vehicle campsites: There are multiple vehicle pullouts that can be used for camping on the approach road and along other roads in the surrounding area up and down UT 95.

Don't Build Fire Rings

32 Sundance Trail (Hike)

A challenging route into "The Grand Canyon of Utah."

Don't Bust the Crust

Start: Sundance Trailhead
Distance: 8.8 miles out and back
Elevation gain: 1,700 feet, mostly on return
Hiking time: 5–8 hours
Difficulty: Difficult, due to steep and demanding talus slope and elevation gain
Trail surface: Sand, dirt, and rocks
Best season: Spring and fall, when dry
Canine compatibility: Leashed dogs allowed
Fees and permits: None
MAPS: USGS topo maps: Indian Head Pass, Utah; **Other maps:** National Geographic Trails Illustrated #703, Manti-La Sal National Forest
Trail contacts: BLM Monticello Field Office, 365 N. Main, PO Box 7, Monticello, UT 84535, (435) 587-1500, www.blm.gov/office/monticello-field-office; **Other (seasonal):** Kane Gulch Ranger Station, UT 261, 4 miles south of UT 95. The Sundance Trail crosses into Glen Canyon National Recreation Area: GCRA, PO Box 1507, Page, AZ 86040, (928) 608-6200. However, the trailhead is administered by the BLM, who can usually answer any questions you might have.
Finding the trailhead: From the town of Blanding, take US 191 south for about 3 miles and turn right onto UT 95. Follow UT 95 west for 67.6 miles to the White Canyon Bridge, inside Glen Canyon National Recreation Area. Cross the bridge and stay on UT 95 for another 0.5 mile, and then turn right just short of milepost 53 onto dirt San Juan CR (SJC) 2731. Follow SJC 2731 for 4.8 miles, then turn right onto SJC 2081. Stay on SJC 2081 through several junctions for 4.3 miles, then turn left onto SJC 256. At 3.3 miles, turn left onto SJC 2821, signed for Sundance Trailhead. Follow SJC 2821 the rough last 1.2 miles to an open slickrock parking area with an information board and trail register. These dirt roads are generally passable to standard 2WD vehicles when dry.
GPS coordinates: N37° 50.85780' / W110° 11.45760'

Top of the rockslide descent.

The Hike

Dark Canyon reaches more than 1,500 feet deep and its main channel is more than 40 miles long. Running from Elk Ridge to the Colorado River, its vast network of tributaries drains a huge area of mountains, highlands, and deserts. Thanks to its size, many people call it "The Grand Canyon of Utah"—but don't expect the kind of development you would find at any national park.

The challenging Sundance Trail offers one of the few ways to access the canyon's lower reaches, descending a giant rockslide from the rim to the floor. The trail is no route for novices, but if you are up to the challenge it can take you into a canyon like no other.

Look for the trailhead next to the brown BLM sign on the north side of the parking area, opposite the information board. The first section of the hike is on a dirt road, which skirts the head of an unnamed draw. The rough road has some sand pits and steep drops, making the going difficult at times.

Approaching Dark Canyon below the Orange Cliffs.

Flowing stream at the bottom of Dark Canyon.

After 0.8 mile the trail wraps around to the west at a viewpoint that reveals both the full scale and depth of Dark Canyon and the massive talus field on the far side of the draw that provides the way down.

Continue on the road around the head of the draw, with views of the Henry Mountains rising sharply to the west. At 1.8 miles a singletrack branches off from the road to the right, marked with a vertical BLM trail sign. Follow a chain of cairns across several flats and down a series of sandstone ledges for 1.5 miles to reach the top of the descent, a dizzying wall of scree dropping straight to the canyon floor. From the top, it is impossible to see more than the first few steps of the route, a disconcerting experience for some hikers.

The way down has a "choose-your-own-adventure" vibe; there is no maintained trail or even a single established route. A proliferation of cairns marks multiple channels down through the scree. Be sure to always keep the next cairn in sight to stay on track. If you can no longer see any cairns, you are likely off the route and should retrace your steps. At times the footing can be loose and intimidating. At other times the footing is firm—but still intimidating.

Unlike the depths of Dark Canyon, which are frequently shaded by the towering rock walls, this slope is almost always in the sun. In the heat of the day, you might well wish it wasn't, especially on the climb back out.

However, that exposure is not the source of the trail's name, which is a shortened version of "The Butch and Sundance Trail," after Butch Cassidy and the Sundance Kid. The infamous Wild Bunch Gang hid from the law in some of the canyon country's most forbidding and inaccessible corners, and some local legends tell that Cassidy built this trail in and out of Dark Canyon as a way to evade capture. Other stories maintain that the trail follows an old Native American path or that it was built by early Spanish explorers, and that it may have just been used by Cassidy and his men.

Reach the bottom of the slide after 0.5 mile and then head east along the wash at its base on a much more gradual descent. At 4.1 miles from the trailhead, step out into a large open area. This point lies at a nexus of several large canyons, including Lost Canyon to the south, Lean-To Canyon to the northeast, the unnamed tributary you just came down, and the main channel of Dark Canyon running through the middle.

Pass through the open space on an obvious footpath for another 0.3 mile to the bottom of Dark Canyon, where a perennial stream flows beneath some cottonwoods. This is the turnaround point for day hikers, but it also makes a great base camp for backpackers undertaking multiple-day explorations of the surrounding landscape.

Miles and Directions

0.0 Start at Sundance Trailhead.

0.8 Reach views of talus descent route into Dark Canyon.

1.8 Turn right (east) onto singletrack at junction.

3.3 Start talus slope descent.

3.8 Reach bottom of talus slope.

4.1 Reach open area on canyon floor.

4.4 Reach bottom of Dark Canyon.

8.8 End back at the trailhead.

Special precautions: Be sure to bring plenty of water on this hike. If you plan on using the stream in Dark Canyon as a water source, a treatment method must be carried as well.

Mountain biking options: It is possible to ride the first part of the route on the dirt road between the trailhead and the start of the singletrack at 1.8 miles, with some hike-a-bike sections. Otherwise, the network of dirt roads between UT 95 and the trailhead offers great opportunities for days of bicycle exploration.

Vehicle campsites: There are multiple vehicle pullouts and other areas for camping all along the approach roads and other roads in the surrounding area.

Don't Build Fire Rings

Backpacking options: Although the Sundance Trail is described here as a day hike, it is also a great access route for extended backpacking trips into lower Dark Canyon. You can use the campsites and reliable water at the end of the trail as a base camp for exploration into all the surrounding canyons, including the 6-mile out-and-back trip to the Colorado River at Cataract Canyon. The route to the river is physically demanding and contains some tricky sections, but there are multiple swimming holes and waterfalls in the

Sundance Trail

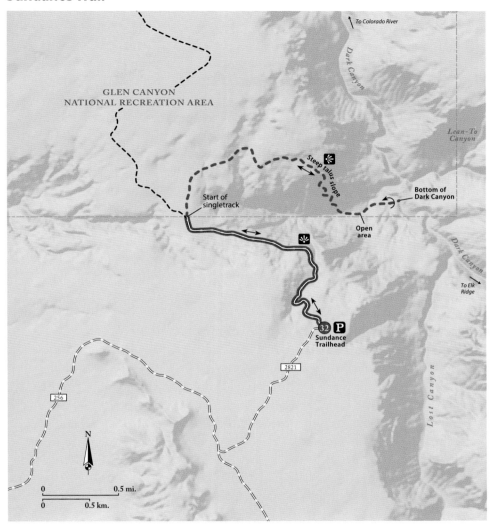

flowing creek along the way. Note that in high flood times Lake Powell can rise high enough to fill the lower floor of Dark Canyon and prevent passage all the way to the end.

Camp & Eat Away from Archaeology

The Art of Hiking

When standing nose to nose with a mountain lion, you're probably not too concerned with the issue of ethical behavior in the wild. No doubt you're just terrified. But let's be honest. How often are you nose to nose with a mountain lion? For most of us, a hike into the "wild" means loading up the SUV with expensive gear and driving to a toileted trailhead. Sure, you can mourn how civilized we've become—how GPS units have replaced natural instinct and Gore-Tex, true-grit—but the silly gadgets of civilization aside, we have plenty of reason to take pride in how we've matured. With survival now on the back burner, we've begun to reason— and it's about time—that we have a responsibility to protect, no longer just conquer, our wild places: that they, not we, are at risk. So please, do what you can. The following section will help you understand better what it means to "do what you can" while still making the most of your hiking experience. Anyone can take a hike, but hiking safely and well is an art requiring preparation and proper equipment.

Reaching the Trailhead

The challenges of some hikes begin before you take a single step. Sometimes, just reaching the trailhead is half the battle. Throughout much of Bears Ears, trailheads and other backcountry access points lie at the end of rough and sandy dirt roads. Most of these roads are passable by standard 2WD vehicles under normal conditions. In the roughest sections, high-clearance is generally more helpful than 4WD. In all cases, cautious driving is the best way to go. If you have any doubts, it's better to get out and scout the route on foot than to blindly drive ahead, hoping for the best.

However, all that changes when the roads get wet. *It doesn't take too much precipitation to turn even the best dirt road in the canyon country into an impassable mire, and no combination of high-clearance, 4WD, or studded tires will save you.* Flash floods can sweep across roadbeds, washing them out at any time. Worse, the hardpack clay that makes up the best part of the roads when dry becomes the worst part when wet. Once saturated, the clay turns into a mucky cement seemingly made up of equal parts grease and glue. Some drivers forge ahead, believing that wet clay

Elaborate anthropomorphic petroglyph panel. JOSH EWING

is no different from mud they may have driven through somewhere else. They are in for a rude awakening. There is no feeling of helplessness quite like your tires instantly gunking up and losing all traction as your vehicle gets caught in an uncontrollable sideways slide. Throw in a nearby cliff edge and the helplessness soon gives way to terror.

Know the weather forecast before you go, and be aware of the conditions over the previous few days. In the spring, snowmelt can cause the same road closures as rain, even in sunny weather. Be aware, too, that if a front is coming in you may have no difficulty reaching your destination but might get trapped there for several days, unable to get back out. ***Your best bet is to check with local sources like the rangers at Kane Gulch for up-to-date road and weather information.***

You're always better safe than sorry. Roads tend to dry out quickly with some exposure to the sun and wind. Wait for another day if you have to. Consider that if you do get stuck somewhere and need to be towed out, it will cost you hundreds of dollars just to have someone come and take a look—and that's if you're lucky enough to have a phone signal.

Trail Etiquette

Zero impact. Always leave an area just like you found it—if not better than you found it. Avoid camping in fragile, alpine meadows and along the banks of streams and lakes. The desert is a harsh landscape, but it is also surprisingly fragile, so always treat it with care. Use a camp stove versus building a wood fire. Pack out all your trash and extra food. Bury human waste at least 100 feet from water sources under 6 to 8 inches of topsoil. Don't bathe with soap in a lake or stream—use prepackaged moistened towels to wipe off sweat and dirt, or bathe in the water without soap.

Visit with respect. The Visit with Respect principles laid out in the Introduction are the key to enjoying and protecting the unique cultural and natural resources of the Bears Ears landscape.

Stay on the trail. It's true, a path anywhere leads nowhere new, but purists will just have to get over it. Paths serve an important purpose; they limit impact on natural areas. Straying from a designated trail may seem innocent, but it can cause damage to sensitive areas—damage that may take years to recover, if it can recover at all. Even simple shortcuts can be destructive. So, please, stay on the trail. In places where there is no trail, stay on the hard slickrock. Always avoid stepping on and crushing cryptobiotic soil, easily identified by its raised, black, sponge-like appearance.

Leave no weeds. Noxious weeds tend to overtake other plants, which in turn affects animals and birds that depend on them for food. To minimize the spread of noxious weeds, hikers should regularly clean their boots, tents, packs, and hiking poles of mud and seeds. Also brush your dog to remove any weed seeds before heading off into a new area.

Keep your dog under control. You can buy a flexi-lead that allows your dog to go exploring along the trail, while allowing you the ability to reel him in should another hiker approach or should he decide to chase a rabbit. Always obey leash laws and be sure to bury your dog's waste or pack it in resealable plastic bags. Although dogs are allowed in some places in Bears Ears, dogs and archaeology don't mix, so it is often best to leave your canine friend at home.

Respect other trail users. Often you're not the only one on the trail. With the rise in popularity of multiuse trails, you'll have to learn a new kind of respect, beyond the nod and "hello" approach you may be used to. First investigate whether you're on a multiuse trail, and assume the appropriate precautions. When you encounter motorized vehicles (ATVs, motorcycles, and 4WDs), be alert. Though they should always yield to the hiker, often they're going too fast or are too lost in the buzz of their engine to react to your presence. If you hear activity ahead, step off the trail just to be safe. Note that you're not likely to hear a mountain biker coming, so be prepared and know ahead of time whether you share the trail with them. Cyclists should always yield to hikers, but that's little comfort to the hiker. Be aware. When you approach horses or pack animals on the trail, always step quietly off the trail, preferably on the downhill side, and let them pass. If you're wearing a large backpack, it's often a good idea to sit down. To some animals, a hiker wearing a large backpack might appear threatening. Many national forests allow domesticated grazing, usually for sheep and cattle. Make sure your dog doesn't harass these animals, and respect ranchers' rights while you're enjoying yours.

Getting into Shape

Unless you want to be sore—and possibly have to shorten your trip or vacation—be sure to get in shape before a big hike. If you're terribly out of shape, start a walking program early, preferably eight weeks in advance. Start with a fifteen-minute walk during your lunch hour or after work and

Ancestral Puebloan structures under dramatic light. JOSH EWING

gradually increase your walking time to an hour. You should also increase your elevation gain. Walking briskly up hills really strengthens your leg muscles and gets your heart rate up. If you work in a storied office building, take the stairs instead of the elevator. If you prefer going to a gym, walk the treadmill or use a stair machine. You can further increase your strength and endurance by walking with a loaded backpack. Stationary exercises you might consider are squats, leg lifts, sit-ups, and push-ups. Other good ways to get in shape include biking, running, aerobics, and, of course, short hikes. Stretching before and after a hike keeps muscles flexible and helps avoid injuries.

Preparedness

It's been said that failing to plan means planning to fail. So do take the necessary time to plan your trip. Whether going on a short day hike or an extended backpack trip, always prepare for the worst. Simply remembering to pack a copy of the *US Army Survival Manual* is not preparedness. Although it's not a bad idea if you plan on entering truly wild places, it's merely the tourniquet answer to a problem. You need to do your best to prevent the problem from arising in the first place. In order to survive—and to stay reasonably comfortable—you need to concern yourself with the basics: water, food, and shelter. Don't go on a hike without having these bases covered. And don't go on a hike expecting to find these items in the woods.

Water. Even in frigid conditions, you need at least two quarts of water a day to function efficiently. Add heat and taxing terrain and you can bump that figure up to one gallon. That's simply a base to work from—your metabolism and your level of conditioning can raise or lower that amount. Unless you know your level, assume that you need one gallon of water a day. In the desert or at high altitude (Bears Ears offers both!), your water usage may increase dramatically without your knowing. You may only realize how much you have lost through sweat when you see the salt stains on your clothes. Now, where do you plan on getting the water?

Preferably not from natural water sources. These sources can be loaded with intestinal disturbers, such as bacteria, viruses, and fertilizers. *Giardia lamblia*, the most common of these disturbers, is a protozoan parasite that lives part of its life cycle as a cyst in water. The parasite spreads when mammals defecate in water sources. Once ingested, giardia can induce cramping, diarrhea, vomiting, and fatigue within two days to two weeks after ingestion. Giardiasis is treatable with prescription drugs. If you believe you've contracted giardiasis, see a doctor immediately.

Many springs in the canyon country are unreliable. Water may be available only during the right season or only for a few days after it rains. Always check with local sources, like the BLM rangers at Kane Gulch, if you plan to collect and use water in the backcountry.

Treating water. The best and easiest solution to avoid polluted water is to carry your water with you. Yet, depending on the nature of your hike and the duration, this may not be an option—one gallon of water weighs 8.5 pounds, making it extremely difficult to carry enough for a multiday backpacking trip. In that case, you'll need to look into treating water. Regardless of which method you choose, you should always carry some water with you in case of an emergency. Save this reserve until you absolutely need it.

There are four methods of treating water: boiling, chemical treatment, ultraviolet (UV) purification, and filtering. If you boil water, it's recommended that you do so for 10 to 15 minutes. This is often impractical because you're forced to exhaust a great deal of your fuel supply. You can opt for chemical treatment, which will kill giardia but will not take care of other chemical pollutants. Another drawback to chemical treatments is the unpleasant taste of the water after it's treated. You can remedy this by adding powdered drink mix to the water. UV purification uses UV light to kill any pathogens in the water and has no bad side effects, but the process is energy intensive so it is often necessary to carry a large number of heavy batteries into the field. Filters are the preferred method for treating water. Many filters remove giardia and organic and inorganic contaminants, and don't leave an aftertaste. Water filters are far from perfect, however, as they can easily become clogged or leak if a gasket wears out. It's always a good idea to carry a backup supply of chemical treatment tablets in case your filter decides to quit on you.

Note that all of these methods *purify* the water, but they cannot *clean* the water. Silty water is common in the canyon country and none of these methods can fix that. Strategies for dealing with heavy silt include pouring the water through a cloth or leaving it in a pot overnight for the silt to settle out, but these only reduce the siltiness without eradicating it.

Food. If we're talking about survival, you can go days without food, as long as you have water. But we're also talking about comfort. Try to avoid foods that are high in sugar and fat like candy bars and potato chips. These food types are harder to digest and are low in nutritional value. Instead, bring along foods that are easy to pack, nutritious, and high in energy (e.g., bagels, nutrition bars, dehydrated fruit, gorp, and jerky). If you are on an overnight trip, easy-to-fix dinners include rice mixes, dehydrated potatoes, pasta with cheese sauce, and soup mixes. For a tasty breakfast, you can fix hot oatmeal with brown sugar and reconstituted milk powder topped off with banana chips. If you like a hot drink in the morning, bring along herbal tea bags or hot chocolate. If you are a coffee junkie, you can purchase coffee that is packaged like tea bags. You can prepackage all your meals in heavy-duty resealable plastic bags to keep food from spilling in your pack. These bags can be reused to pack out trash.

Shelter. The type of shelter you choose depends less on the conditions than on your tolerance for discomfort. Shelter comes in many forms—tent, tarp, lean-to, bivy sack, cabin, cave, and so on. If you're camping in the desert, a bivy sack may suffice, but if you're above the tree line and a storm is approaching, a better choice is a three- or four-season tent. Tents are the logical and most popular choice for most backpackers as they're lightweight and packable—and you can rest assured that you always have shelter from the elements. Before you leave on your trip, anticipate what the weather and terrain will be like and plan for the type of shelter that will work best for your comfort level (see Equipment later in this section).

Finding a campsite. If there are established campsites, stick to those. If not, start looking for a campsite early—around 3:30 or 4 p.m. Stop at the first decent site you see. Depending on the area, it could be a long time before you find another suitable location. Pitch your camp in an area that's level. Make sure the area is at least 200 feet from fragile areas like lakeshores, meadows, and stream banks. And try to avoid areas thick in underbrush, as they can harbor insects and provide cover for approaching animals.

If you are camping in stormy, rainy weather, look for a rock outcrop or a shelter in the trees to keep the wind from blowing your tent all night. Be sure that you don't camp under trees with dead limbs that might break off on top of you. Also, try to find an area that has an absorbent surface, such as sandy soil or forest duff. This, in addition to camping on a surface with a slight angle, will provide better drainage. By all means, don't dig trenches to provide drainage around your tent—remember you're practicing zero-impact camping.

If you're in bear country, steer clear of creek beds or animal paths. If you see any signs of a bear's presence (e.g., scat, footprints), relocate. You'll need to find a campsite near a tall tree where you can hang your food and other items that may attract bears such as deodorant, toothpaste, or soap. Carry a lightweight nylon rope with which to hang your food. As a rule, you should hang your food at least 20 feet from the ground and 5 feet away from the tree trunk. You can put food and other items in a waterproof stuff sack and tie one end of the rope to the stuff sack. To get the other end of the rope over the tree branch, tie a good-size rock to it and gently toss the rock over the tree branch. Pull the stuff sack up until it reaches the top of the branch and tie it off securely. Don't hang your food near your tent! If possible, hang your food at least 100 feet away from your campsite. Alternatives to hanging your food are bear-proof plastic tubes and metal bear boxes.

Lastly, think of comfort. Lie down on the ground where you intend to sleep and see if it's a good fit. For morning warmth (and a nice view to wake up to), have your tent face east.

First Aid

I know you're tough, but get 10 miles into the woods and develop a blister and you'll wish you had carried that first-aid kit. Face it, it's just plain good sense. Many companies produce lightweight, compact first-aid kits. Just make sure yours contains at least the following:
- adhesive bandages
- moleskin or duct tape
- various sterile gauze and dressings
- white surgical tape
- an Ace bandage
- an antihistamine
- aspirin, ibuprofen, or acetaminophen
- Betadine solution
- a first-aid book
- antacid tablets
- tweezers
- scissors
- antibacterial wipes
- triple-antibiotic ointment

- plastic gloves
- sterile cotton tip applicators
- syrup of ipecac (to induce vomiting)
- thermometer
- wire splint

Here are a few tips for dealing with and hopefully preventing certain ailments.

Sunburn. Much of Bears Ears is at high elevation with limited shade, so sunburns are particularly easy to get. Take along sunscreen or sunblock, protective clothing, and a wide-brimmed hat. If you do get a sunburn, treat the area with aloe vera gel, and protect the area from further sun exposure. At higher elevations, the sun's radiation can be particularly damaging to skin. Remember that your eyes are vulnerable to this radiation as well. Sunglasses can be a good way to prevent headaches and permanent eye damage from the sun, especially in places where light-colored rock or patches of snow reflect light up in your face.

Blisters. Be prepared to take care of these hike-spoilers by carrying moleskin (a lightly padded adhesive), gauze and tape, or adhesive bandages. An effective way to apply moleskin is to cut out a circle of moleskin and remove the center—like a doughnut—and place it over the blistered area. Cutting the center out will reduce the pressure applied to the sensitive skin. Other products can help combat blisters. Some are applied to suspicious hot spots before a blister forms to help decrease friction to that area, while others are applied to the blister after it has popped to help prevent further irritation.

Insect bites and stings. You can treat most insect bites and stings by applying hydrocortisone 1% cream topically and taking a pain medication such as ibuprofen or acetaminophen to reduce swelling. If you forgot to pack these items, a cold compress or a paste of mud and ashes can sometimes assuage the itching and discomfort. Remove any stingers by using tweezers or scraping the area with your fingernail or a knife blade. Don't pinch the area as you'll only spread the venom.

Some hikers are highly sensitive to bites and stings and may have a serious allergic reaction that can be life threatening. Symptoms of a serious allergic reaction can include wheezing, an asthmatic attack, and shock. The treatment for this severe type of reaction is epinephrine. If you know that you are sensitive to bites and stings, carry a prepackaged

Fish Canyon reflection.

kit of epinephrine, which can be obtained only by prescription from your doctor.

Ticks. Ticks can carry diseases such as Rocky Mountain spotted fever and Lyme disease. The best defense is, of course, prevention. If you know you're going to be hiking through an area littered with ticks, wear long pants and a long-sleeved shirt. You can apply a permethrin repellent to your clothing and a DEET repellent to exposed skin. At the end of your hike, do a spot check for ticks (and insects in general). If you do find a tick, coat the insect with petroleum jelly or tree sap to cut off its air supply. The tick should release its hold, but if it doesn't, grab the head of the tick firmly—with a pair of tweezers if you have them—and gently pull it away from the skin with a twisting motion. Sometimes the mouth parts linger, embedded in your skin. If this happens, try to remove them with a disinfected needle. Clean the affected area with an antibacterial cleanser and then apply triple-antibiotic ointment. Monitor the area for a few days. If irritation persists or a white spot develops, see a doctor for possible infection.

Poison ivy, oak, and sumac. These skin irritants can be found most anywhere in North America and come in the form of a bush or a vine, having leaflets in groups of three, five, seven, or nine. Learn how to spot the plants. The oil they secrete can cause an allergic reaction in the form of blisters, usually about 12 hours after exposure. The itchy rash can last from ten days to several weeks. The best defense against these irritants is to wear clothing that covers the arms, legs, and torso. For summer, zip-off cargo pants come in handy. There are also nonprescription lotions you can apply to exposed skin that guard against the effects of poison ivy/oak/sumac and can be washed off with soap and water. If you think you were in contact with the plants, after hiking (or even on the trail during longer hikes) wash with soap and water. Taking a hot shower with soap after you return home from your hike will also help remove any lingering oil from your skin. Should you contract a rash from any of these plants, use an antihistamine to reduce the itching. If the rash is localized, create a light bleach/water wash to dry up the area. If the rash has spread, either tough it out or see your doctor about getting a dose of cortisone (available both orally and by injection).

Snakebites. Snakebites are rare in North America. Unless startled or provoked, the majority of snakes will not bite. If you are wise to their habitats and keep a careful eye on the trail, you should be just fine. When stepping over logs, first step on the log, making sure you can see what's on the other side before stepping down. Though your chances of being struck are slim, it's wise to know what to do in the event you are.

If a *nonpoisonous* snake bites you, allow the wound to bleed a small amount and then cleanse the wounded area with a Betadine solution (10% povidone iodine). Rinse the wound with clean water (preferably) or fresh urine (it might sound ugly, but it's sterile). Once the area is clean, cover it with triple-antibiotic ointment and a clean bandage. Remember, most residual damage from snakebites, poisonous or otherwise, comes from infection, not the snake's venom. Keep the area as clean as possible and get medical attention immediately.

If you are bitten by a *poisonous* snake, remove the toxin with a suctioning device, found in a snakebite kit. If you do not have such a device, squeeze the wound—*do not* use your mouth for suction, as the venom will enter your bloodstream through the vessels under the tongue and head straight for your heart. Then clean the wound just as you would a nonpoisonous bite. Tie a clean band of cloth snuggly around the afflicted appendage, about an inch or so above the bite (or the rim of the swelling). This is *not* a tourniquet—you want to simply slow the blood flow, not cut it off. Loosen the band if numbness ensues. Remove the band for a minute and reapply a little higher every 10 minutes.

If it is your friend who's been bitten, treat him or her for shock—make the person comfortable, have him or her lie down, elevate the legs, and keep him or her warm. Avoid applying anything cold to the bite wound. Immobilize the affected area and remove any constricting items such as rings, watches, or restrictive clothing—swelling may occur. Once your friend is stable and relatively calm, hike out to get help. The victim should get treatment within 12 hours, ideally, which usually consists of a tetanus shot, antivenin, and antibiotics.

If you are alone and struck by a poisonous snake, stay calm. Hysteria will only quicken the venom's spread. Follow the procedure above, and do your best to reach help. When hiking out, don't run—you'll only increase the flow of blood throughout your system. Instead, walk calmly.

Dehydration. Have you ever hiked in hot weather and had a roaring headache and felt fatigued after only a few miles? More than likely you were dehydrated. Symptoms of dehydration include fatigue, headache, and decreased coordination and judgment. When you are hiking, your body's rate of fluid loss depends on the outside temperature, humidity, altitude, and your activity level. On average, a hiker walking in warm weather will lose four liters of fluid a day. That fluid loss is easily replaced by normal consumption of liquids and food. However, if a hiker is walking briskly in hot, dry weather and hauling a heavy pack, he or she can lose one to three liters of water an hour. It's important to always carry plenty of water and to stop often and drink fluids regularly, even if you aren't thirsty. Dehydration is a particularly salient risk in the dry desert and at high altitude—and Bears Ears is both.

Heat exhaustion is the result of a loss of large amounts of electrolytes and often occurs if a hiker is dehydrated and has been under heavy exertion. Common symptoms of heat exhaustion include cramping, exhaustion, fatigue, lightheadedness, and nausea. You can treat heat exhaustion by getting out of the sun and drinking an electrolyte solution made up of one teaspoon of salt and one tablespoon of sugar dissolved in a liter of water. Drink this solution slowly over a period of one hour. Drinking plenty of fluids (preferably an electrolyte solution/sports drink) can prevent heat exhaustion. Avoid hiking during the hottest parts of the day, and wear breathable clothing, a wide-brimmed hat, and sunglasses.

Hypothermia is one of the biggest dangers in the backcountry, especially for day hikers in the desert. That may sound strange, but imagine starting out on a hike in spring when it's sunny and 80 degrees out. You're clad in nylon shorts and a cotton T-shirt. About halfway through your hike, the sky begins to cloud up, and in the next hour a light drizzle begins to fall and the wind starts to pick up. Before you know it, you are soaking wet and shivering—the perfect recipe for hypothermia. More advanced signs include decreased coordination, slurred speech, and blurred vision. When a victim's temperature falls below 92 degrees, the blood pressure and pulse plummet, possibly leading to coma and death.

To avoid hypothermia, always bring a windproof/rainproof shell, a fleece jacket, tights made of a breathable synthetic fiber, gloves, and hat when you are hiking in the mountains. Learn to adjust your clothing layers based on the temperature. If you are climbing uphill at a moderate pace you will stay warm, but when you stop for a break you'll become cold quickly, unless you add more layers of clothing.

If a hiker is showing advanced signs of hypothermia, dress him or her in dry clothes and make sure he or she is wearing a hat and gloves. Place the person in a sleeping bag in a tent or shelter that will protect him or her from the wind and other elements. Give the person warm fluids to drink and keep him or her awake.

Frostbite. When the mercury dips below 32 degrees, your extremities begin to chill. If a persistent chill attacks a localized area, say, your hands or your toes, the circulatory system reacts by cutting off blood flow to the affected area—the idea being to protect and preserve the body's overall temperature. And so it's death by attrition for the affected area. Ice crystals start to form from the water in the cells of the neglected tissue. Deprived of heat, nourishment, and now water, the tissue literally starves. This is frostbite.

Prevention is your best defense against this situation. Most prone to frostbite are your face, hands, and feet, so protect these areas well. Wool is the material of choice because it provides ample air space for insulation and draws moisture away from the skin. Synthetic fabrics, however, have recently made great strides in the cold weather clothing market. Do your research. A pair of light silk liners under your regular gloves is a good trick for keeping warm. They afford some additional warmth, but more important they'll allow you to remove your mitts for tedious work without exposing the skin.

If your feet or hands start to feel cold or numb due to the elements, warm them as quickly as possible. Place cold hands under your armpits or bury them in your crotch. If your feet are cold, change your socks. If there's plenty of room in your boots, add another pair of socks. Do remember, though, that constricting your feet in tight boots can restrict blood flow and actually make your feet colder more quickly. Your socks need to have breathing room if they're going to be effective. Dead air provides insulation. If your face is cold, place your warm hands over your face, or simply wear a head stocking.

Should your skin go numb and start to appear white and waxy, chances are you've got or are developing frostbite. Don't try to thaw the area unless you can maintain the warmth. In other words, don't stop to warm up your frostbitten feet only to head back on the trail. You'll do more damage than good. Tests have shown that hikers who walked on thawed feet did more harm, and endured more pain, than hikers who left the affected areas alone. Do your best to get out of the cold entirely and seek medical attention—which usually consists of performing a rapid rewarming in water for 20 to 30 minutes.

The overall objective in preventing both hypothermia and frostbite is to keep the body's core warm. Protect key areas where heat escapes, like the top of the head, and maintain the proper nutrition level. Foods that are high in calories aid the body in producing heat. Never smoke or drink when you're in situations where the cold is threatening. By affecting blood flow, these activities ultimately cool the body's core temperature.

Altitude sickness (AMS). High lofty peaks, clear alpine lakes, and vast mountain views beckon hikers to the high country. But those who like to venture high may become victims of altitude sickness (also known as Acute Mountain Sickness—AMS). Altitude sickness is your body's reaction to insufficient oxygen in the blood due to decreased barometric pressure. While some hikers may feel lightheaded, nauseous, and experience shortness of breath at 7,000 feet, others may not experience these symptoms until they reach 10,000 feet or higher.

Slowing your ascent to high places and giving your body a chance to acclimatize to the higher elevations can prevent altitude sickness. For example, if you live at sea level and are planning a weeklong backpacking trip to elevations between 7,000 and 12,000 feet, start by staying below 7,000 feet for one night, then move to between 7,000 and 10,000 feet for another night or two. Avoid strenuous exertion and alcohol to give your body a chance to adjust to the new altitude. It's also important to eat light food and drink plenty of nonalcoholic fluids, preferably water. Loss of appetite at altitude is common, but you must eat!

Most hikers who experience mild to moderate AMS develop a headache and/or nausea, grow lethargic, and have problems sleeping. The treatment for AMS is simple: stop heading uphill. Keep eating and drinking water and take meds for the headache. You actually need to take more breaths at altitude than at sea level, so breathe a little faster without hyperventilating. If symptoms don't improve over 24 to 48 hours, descend. Once a victim descends about 2,000 to 3,000 feet, his or her signs will usually begin to diminish.

Severe AMS comes in two forms: High Altitude Pulmonary Edema (HAPE) and High Altitude Cerebral Edema (HACE). HAPE, an accumulation of fluid in the lungs, can occur above 8,000 feet. Symptoms include rapid heart rate, shortness of breath at rest, AMS symptoms, dry cough developing into a wet cough, gurgling sounds, flu-like or bronchitis symptoms, and lack of muscle coordination. HAPE is life threatening, so descend immediately, at least 2,000 to 4,000 feet. HACE usually occurs above 12,000 feet but sometimes occurs above 10,000 feet. Symptoms are similar to HAPE but also include seizures, hallucinations, paralysis, and vision disturbances. Descend immediately—HACE is also life threatening.

Sunlight through cottonwoods.

House on Fire in winter. JOSH EWING

Hantavirus Pulmonary Syndrome (HPS). Deer mice spread the virus that causes HPS, and humans contract it from breathing it in, usually when they've disturbed an area with dust and mice feces from nests or surfaces with mice droppings or urine. Exposure to large numbers of rodents and their feces or urine presents the greatest risk. Hikers sometimes enter old buildings or ruins, and often deer mice live in these places. This is another good reason to stay out! About half the people who develop HPS die. Symptoms are flu-like and appear about two to three weeks after exposure. After initial symptoms, a dry cough and shortness of breath follow. Breathing is difficult. If you even think you might have HPS, see a doctor immediately!

Natural Hazards

Besides tripping over a rock or tree root on the trail, which can easily lead to a catastrophic fall over a cliff or the edge of a canyon, there are some other real hazards to be aware of while hiking. Even if where you're hiking doesn't have the plethora of poisonous snakes and plants, insects, and grizzly bears found in other parts of the United States, there are a few weather conditions and predators you may need to take into account.

Cactus spines. Prickly pear, barrel, and other types of cacti are abundant in the desert canyons of southern Utah, and even just brushing against one can result in painful and irritating spines lodged in the skin. Stripping the spines out with duct tape is a common field solution, but this is not typically effective for removing a majority of the spines. A better solution is to carry a set of tweezers and a pair of work gloves for pulling them out.

Lightning. Thunderstorms build over the mountains almost every day during the summer. Lightning is generated by thunderheads and can strike without warning, even several miles away from the nearest overhead cloud. The best rule of thumb is to start leaving exposed peaks, ridges, and canyon rims by about noon. This time can vary a little depending on storm buildup. Keep an eye on cloud formation, and don't underestimate how fast a storm can build. The bigger they get, the more likely a thunderstorm will happen. Lightning takes the path of least resistance, so if you're the high point, it might choose you. Ducking under a rock overhang is dangerous, as you form the shortest path between the rock and ground. If you dash below tree line, avoid standing under the only or the tallest tree. If you are caught above tree line, stay away from anything metal you might be carrying. Move down off the ridge slightly to a low, treeless point and squat until the storm passes. If you have an insulating pad, squat on it. Avoid having both your hands and feet touching the ground at once and never lay flat. If you hear a buzzing sound or feel your hair standing on end, move quickly because an electrical charge is building up.

Flash floods. On July 31, 1976, a torrential downpour unleashed by a thunderstorm dumped tons of water into the Big Thompson watershed near Estes Park. Within hours, a wall of water moved down the narrow canyon, killing 139 people and causing more than $30 million in property damage. The spooky thing about flash floods, especially in western canyons, is that they can appear out of nowhere from a storm many miles away. While hiking or driving in canyons, keep an eye on the weather. Always climb to safety if danger threatens. Flash floods usually subside quickly, so be patient and don't cross a swollen stream or wash. Amazingly, one of the biggest causes of death in the desert is drowning(!) due to flash flooding, so always be aware of the weather and your surroundings, especially when hiking in the confined walls of a canyon.

Bears. Most of the United States (outside of the Pacific Northwest and parts of the Northern Rockies) does not have a grizzly bear population, although some rumors exist about sightings where there should be none. Black bears are plentiful, however. Here are some tips in case you and a bear scare each other. Most of all, avoid scaring a bear. Watch for bear tracks (five toes) and droppings (sizable with leaves, partly digested berries, seeds, and/or animal fur). Talk or sing where visibility or hearing are limited. Keep a clean camp, hang food, and don't sleep in the clothes you wore while cooking. Be especially careful in spring to avoid getting between a mother and her cubs. In late summer and fall bears are busy eating berries and acorns to fatten up for winter, so be extra careful around berry bushes and oakbrush. If you do encounter a bear, move away slowly while facing the bear, talk softly, and avoid direct eye contact. Give the bear room to escape. Since bears are very curious, it might stand upright to get a better whiff of you, and it may even charge you to try to intimidate you. Try to stay calm. If a bear does attack you, fight back with anything you have handy. Unleashed dogs have been known to come running back to their owners with a bear close behind. Keep your dog on a leash or leave him at home.

Mountain lions. Mountain lions appear to be getting more comfortable around humans as long as deer (their favorite prey) are in an area with adequate cover. Usually elusive and quiet, lions rarely attack people. If you meet a lion, give it a chance to escape. Stay calm and talk firmly to it. Back away slowly while facing the lion. If you run, you'll only encourage the curious cat to chase you. Make yourself look large by opening a jacket, if you have one, or waving your hiking poles. If the lion behaves aggressively throw stones, sticks, or whatever you can while remaining tall. If a lion does attack, fight for your life with anything you can grab.

Moose. Because moose have very few natural predators, they don't fear humans like other animals. You might find moose in sagebrush and wetter areas of willow, aspen, and pine, or in beaver habitats. Mothers with calves, as well as bulls during mating season, can be particularly aggressive. If a moose threatens you, back away slowly and talk calmly to it. Keep your dog away from moose.

Other considerations. Hunting is a popular sport in the United States, especially during rifle season in October and November. Hiking is still enjoyable in those months in many areas, so just take a few precautions. First, learn when the different hunting seasons start and end in the area in which you'll be hiking. During this time frame, be sure to wear at least a blaze orange hat, and possibly put an orange vest over your pack. Don't be surprised to see hunters in camo outfits carrying bows or muzzle-loading rifles around during their season. If you would feel more comfortable without hunters around, hike in national parks and monuments or state and local parks where hunting is not allowed.

Navigation

Whether you are going on a short hike in a familiar area or planning a weeklong backpack trip, you should always be equipped with the proper navigational equipment—at the very least a detailed map and a sturdy compass.

Maps. There are many different types of maps available to help you find your way on the trail. Easiest to find are Forest Service maps and BLM (Bureau of Land Management) maps. These maps tend to cover large areas, so be sure they are detailed enough for your particular trip. You can also obtain national park maps as well as high-quality maps from private companies and trail groups. These maps can be obtained either from outdoor stores or ranger stations.

US Geological Survey topographic maps are particularly popular with hikers—especially serious backcountry hikers. These maps contain the standard map symbols such as roads, lakes, and rivers, as well as contour lines that show the details of the trail terrain like ridges, valleys, passes,

The tortuous channel of Grand Gulch.

and mountain peaks. The 7.5-minute series (1 inch on the map equals approximately 2/5 mile on the ground) provides the closest inspection available. USGS maps are available by mail (US Geological Survey, Map Distribution Branch, P.O. Box 25286, Denver, CO 80225) or online at www.usgs.gov/products/maps/topo-maps.

If you want to check out the high-tech world of maps, you can purchase topographic maps online. These software-mapping programs let you select a route on your computer, print it out, then take it with you on the trail. Some software mapping programs let you insert symbols and labels, download waypoints from a GPS unit, and export the maps to other software programs.

The art of map reading is a skill that you can develop by first practicing in an area you are familiar with. To begin, orient the map so it is lined up in the correct direction (i.e., north on the map is lined up with true north). Next, familiarize yourself with the map symbols and try to match them up with terrain features around you such as a high ridge, mountain peak, river, or lake. If you are practicing with a USGS map, notice the contour lines. On gentler terrain these contour lines are spaced farther apart, and on steeper terrain they are closer together. Pick a short loop trail, and stop frequently to check your position on the map. As you practice map reading, you'll learn how to anticipate a steep section on the trail or a good place to take a rest break, and so on.

Compasses. First off, the sun is not a substitute for a compass. So what kind of compass should you have? Here are some characteristics you should look for: a rectangular base with detailed scales; a protective, liquid-filled housing; a sighting line on the mirror; luminous alignment and back-bearing arrows; a luminous north-seeking arrow; and a well-defined bezel ring.

You can learn compass basics by reading the detailed instructions included with your compass. If you want to fine-tune your compass skills, sign up for an orienteering class or purchase a book on compass reading. Once you've learned the basic skills on using a compass, remember to practice these skills before you head into the backcountry.

If you are a klutz at using a compass, you may be interested in checking out the technical wizardry of the GPS (Global Positioning System) device. The GPS was developed by the Pentagon and works off twenty-four NAVSTAR satellites, which were designed to guide missiles to their targets. A GPS device is a handheld unit that calculates your latitude and longitude with the easy press of a button. The Department of Defense used to scramble the satellite signals a bit to prevent civilians (and spies!) from getting extremely accurate readings, but that practice was discontinued in May 2000, and GPS units now provide nearly pinpoint accuracy (within 30 to 60 feet).

There are many different types of GPS units available, and they range in price from $100 to $400. In general, all GPS units have a display screen and keypad where you input information. In addition to acting as a compass, the unit allows you to plot your route, easily retrace your path, track your traveling speed, find the mileage between waypoints, and calculate the total mileage of your route.

Before you purchase a GPS unit, keep in mind that these devices don't pick up signals indoors, in heavily wooded areas, on mountain peaks, or in deep valleys. Although most smartphones now incorporate GPS receivers, they are subject to the same signal-blocking limitations and often have shorter battery lives than a stand-alone receiver would have.

Pedometers. A pedometer is a small, clip-on unit with a digital display that calculates your hiking distance in miles or kilometers based on your walking stride. Some units also calculate the calories you burn and your total hiking time. Pedometers are available at most large outdoor stores and range in price from $20 to $40. There are also multiple smartphone apps that provide similar functionality.

Trip Planning

Planning your hiking adventure begins with letting a friend or relative know your trip itinerary so they can call for help if you don't return at your scheduled time. Your next task is to make sure you are outfitted to experience the risks and rewards of the trail. This section highlights gear and clothing you may want to take with you to get the most out of your hike.

Day Hikes
- camera
- compass/GPS unit
- pedometer
- daypack
- first-aid kit
- fleece jacket
- food

- guidebook
- hat
- headlamp/flashlight with extra batteries and bulbs
- insect repellent
- knife/multipurpose tool
- map
- matches in waterproof container and fire starter
- rain gear
- space blanket
- sunglasses
- sunscreen
- swimsuit
- watch
- water
- water bottles/water hydration system

Overnight Trip
- backpack and waterproof rain cover
- backpacker's trowel
- bandanna
- bear bell
- bear repellent spray
- biodegradable soap
- collapsible water container (2–3 gallon capacity)
- clothing—extra wool socks, shirt, and shorts
- cook set/utensils
- ditty bags to store gear
- extra plastic resealable bags
- gaiters
- garbage bag
- ground cloth
- journal/pen
- long underwear
- nylon rope to hang food
- permit (if required)
- pot scrubber
- rain jacket and pants
- sandals to wear around camp and to ford streams

- sleeping bag with waterproof stuff sack
- sleeping pad
- small bath towel
- stove and fuel
- tent
- toiletry items
- water filter
- whistle

Equipment

With the outdoor market currently flooded with products, many of which are pure gimmickry, it seems impossible to both differentiate and choose. Do I really need a tropical-fish-lined collapsible shower? (No, you don't.) The only defense against the maddening quantity of items thrust in your face is to think practically—and to do so before you go shopping. The worst buys are impulsive buys. Since most name brands will differ only slightly in quality, it's best to know what you're looking for in terms of function. Buy only what you need. You will, don't forget, be carrying what you've bought on your back. Here are some things to keep in mind before you go shopping.

Clothes. Clothing is your armor against Mother Nature's little surprises. Hikers should be prepared for any possibility, especially when hiking in mountainous areas. Adequate rain protection and extra layers of clothing are a good idea. In summer, a wide-brimmed hat can help keep the sun at bay. In the winter months the first layer you'll want to wear is a "wicking" layer of long underwear that keeps perspiration away from your skin. Wear long underwear made from synthetic fibers that wick moisture away from the skin and draw it toward the next layer of clothing, where it then evaporates. Avoid wearing long underwear made of cotton, as it is slow to dry and keeps moisture next to your skin.

The second layer you'll wear is the "insulating" layer. Aside from keeping you warm, this layer needs to "breathe" so you stay dry while hiking. A fabric that provides insulation and dries quickly is fleece. It's interesting to note that this one-of-a-kind fabric is made out of recycled plastic. Purchasing a zip-up jacket made of this material is highly recommended.

The last line of layering defense is the "shell" layer. You'll need some type of waterproof, windproof, breathable jacket that will fit over all of your other layers. It should have a large hood that fits over a hat. You'll also need a good pair of rain pants made from a similar waterproof, breathable fabric. Some Gore-Tex jackets cost as much as $500, but you should know that there are more affordable fabrics out there that work just as well.

Now that you've learned the basics of layering, you can't forget to protect your hands and face. In cold, windy, or rainy weather you'll need a hat made of wool or fleece and insulated, waterproof gloves that will keep your hands warm and toasty. As mentioned earlier, buying an additional pair of light silk liners to wear under your regular gloves is a good idea.

Footwear. If you have any extra money to spend on your trip, put that money into boots or trail shoes. Poor shoes will bring a hike to a halt faster than anything else. To avoid this annoyance, buy shoes that provide support and are lightweight and flexible. A lightweight hiking boot is better than a heavy, leather mountaineering boot for most day hikes and backpacking. Trail running shoes provide a little extra cushion and are made in a high-top style that many people wear for hiking. These running shoes are lighter, more flexible, and more breathable than hiking boots. If you know you'll be hiking in wet weather often, purchase boots or shoes with a Gore-Tex liner, which will help keep your feet dry.

When buying your boots, be sure to wear the same type of socks you'll be wearing on the trail. If the boots you're buying are for cold weather hiking, try the boots on while wearing two pairs of socks. Speaking of socks, a good cold weather sock combination is to wear a thinner sock made of wool or polypropylene covered by a heavier outer sock made of wool. The inner sock protects the foot from the rubbing effects of the outer sock and prevents blisters. Many outdoor stores have some type of ramp to simulate hiking uphill and downhill. Be sure to take advantage of this test, as toe-jamming boot fronts can be very painful and debilitating on the downhill trek.

Once you've purchased your footwear, be sure to break them in before you hit the trail. New footwear is often stiff and needs to be stretched and molded to your foot.

Hiking poles. Use rubber-tipped hiking poles. Hiking poles help with balance, and more important take pressure off your knees. The ones with shock absorbers are easier on your elbows and knees. Some poles even come with a camera attachment to be used as a monopod. And heaven forbid you meet a mountain lion, bear, or unfriendly dog, the poles can make you look a lot bigger.

Use Rubber-Tipped Hiking Poles.

Backpacks. No matter what type of hiking you do you'll need a pack of some sort to carry the basic trail essentials. There are a variety of backpacks on the market, but let's first discuss what you intend to use it for: day hikes or overnight trips?

If you plan on doing a day hike, a daypack should have some of the following characteristics: a padded hip belt that's at least 2 inches in diameter (avoid packs with only a small nylon piece of webbing for a hip belt); a chest strap (the chest strap helps stabilize the pack against your body); external pockets to carry water and other items that you want easy access to; an internal pocket to hold keys, a knife, a wallet, and other miscellaneous items; an external lashing system to hold a jacket; and a hydration pocket for carrying a hydration system (which consists of a water bladder with an attachable drinking hose).

For short hikes, some hikers like to use a fanny pack to store just a camera, food, a compass, a map, and other trail essentials. Most fanny packs have pockets for two water bottles and a padded hip belt.

If you intend to do an extended, overnight trip, there are multiple considerations. First off, you need to decide what kind of framed pack you want. There are two backpack types for backpacking: the internal frame and the external frame. An internal frame pack rests closer to your body, making it more stable and easier to balance when hiking over rough terrain. An external frame pack is just that, an aluminum frame attached to the exterior of the pack. An external frame pack is good for long backpack trips because it distributes the pack weight better and you can carry heavier loads. It's easier to pack, and your gear is more accessible. It also offers better back ventilation in hot weather. However, external frame packs are increasingly rare, replaced by better-designed and newer internal frame packs that are also well suited to carrying heavy loads and often weigh less to begin with.

The most critical measurement for fitting a pack is torso length. The pack needs to rest evenly on your hips without sagging. A good pack will come in two or three sizes and have straps and hip belts that are adjustable according to your body size and characteristics.

When you purchase a backpack, go to an outdoor store with salespeople who are knowledgeable in how to properly fit a pack. Once the pack is fitted for you, load the pack with the amount of weight you plan on taking on the trail. The weight of the pack should be distributed evenly and you should be able to swing your arms and walk briskly without feeling out of balance. Another good technique for evaluating a pack is to walk up and down stairs and make quick turns to the right and to the left to be sure the pack doesn't feel out of balance. Other features that are nice to have on a backpack include a removable daypack or fanny pack, external pockets for extra water, and extra lash points to attach a jacket or other items.

Sleeping bags and pads. Sleeping bags are rated by temperature. You can purchase a bag made of synthetic fiber, or you can buy a goose down bag. Goose down bags are more expensive, but they have a higher insulating capacity by weight and will keep their loft longer. You'll want to purchase a bag with a temperature rating that fits the time of year and conditions you are most likely to camp in. One caveat: The techno-standard for temperature ratings is far from perfect. Ratings vary from manufacturer to manufacturer, so to protect yourself you should purchase a bag rated 10 to 15 degrees below the temperature you expect to be camping in. Synthetic bags are more resistant to water than down bags, but many down bags are now made with a Gore-Tex shell that helps repel water. Down bags are also more compressible than synthetic bags and take up less room in your pack, which is an important consideration if you are planning a multiday backpack trip. Features to look for in a sleeping bag include a mummy-style bag, a hood you can cinch down around your head in cold weather, and draft tubes along the zippers that help keep heat in and drafts out.

You'll also want a sleeping pad to provide insulation and padding from the cold ground. There are different types of sleeping pads available, from the more expensive self-inflating air mattresses to the less expensive closed-cell foam pads. Self-inflating air mattresses, though comfortable, are usually heavier than closed-cell foam mattresses and are prone to punctures.

Tents. The tent is your home away from home while on the trail. It provides protection from wind, snow, rain, and insects. A three-season tent is a good choice for backpacking and can range in price from $100 to $500 or more. These lightweight and versatile tents provide protection in all types of weather, except heavy snowstorms or high winds, and range in weight from four to eight pounds. Look for a tent that's easy to set up and will easily fit two people with gear. Dome-type tents usually offer more headroom and places to store gear. Other tent designs include a vestibule where you can store wet boots and backpacks. Some nice-to-have items in a tent include interior pockets to store small items and lashing points to hang a clothesline. Most three-season tents also come with stakes so you can secure the tent in high winds. Before you purchase a tent, set it up and take it down a few times to be sure it is easy to handle. Also, sit inside the tent and make sure it has enough room for you and your gear.

Cell phones. Many hikers are carrying their cell phones into the backcountry these days in case of emergency. That's fine and good, but please know that cell phone coverage is often poor to nonexistent in valleys, canyons, and thick forest. More important, people have started to call for help because they're tired or lost. Let's go back to being prepared. You are responsible for yourself in the backcountry. Use your brain to avoid problems, and if you do encounter one, first use your brain to try to correct the situation. Only use your cell phone, if it works, in true emergencies.

Hiking with Children

Hiking with children isn't a matter of how many miles you can cover or how much elevation gain you make in a day; it's about seeing and experiencing nature through their eyes.

Kids like to explore and have fun. They like to stop and point out bugs and plants, look under rocks, jump in puddles, and throw sticks. If you're taking a toddler or young child on a hike, start with a trail that you're familiar with. Trails that have interesting things for kids, like piles of leaves to play in or a small stream to wade through during the summer, will make the hike much more enjoyable for them and will keep them from getting bored.

That said, it's important to keep your children's natural desire to explore in check when visiting archaeological sites. A ruin might look like a playground to a child, but you should know better. A collapsing wall from a child trying to climb it both irreparably damages the structure and is a danger to the child. Carefully guide children through sites rather than letting them run rampant. This helps preserve the site and also allows you to pass down valuable **Visit with Respect** messaging to the next generation.

Guide Children Through Sites

You can keep your child's attention if you have a strategy before starting on the trail. Using games is not only an effective way to keep a child's attention, it's also a great way to teach him or her about nature. Play hide and seek, where your child is the mouse and you are the hawk. Quiz children on the names of plants and animals. If your children are old enough, let them carry their own daypack filled with snacks and water. So that you are sure to go at their pace and not yours, let them lead the way. Playing follow the leader works particularly well when you have a group of children. Have each child take a turn at being the leader.

With children, a lot of clothing is key. The only thing predictable about weather is that it will change. Especially in mountainous areas, weather can change dramatically in a very short time. Always bring extra clothing for children, regardless of the season. In the winter, have your children wear wool socks and warm layers such as long underwear, a fleece jacket and hat, wool mittens, and good rain gear. It's not a bad idea to have these along in late fall and early spring as well. Good footwear is also important. A sturdy pair of high-top tennis shoes or lightweight hiking boots are the best bet for little ones. If you're hiking in the summer near a lake or stream, bring along a pair of old sneakers that your child can put on when he or she wants to go exploring in the water. Remember when you're near any type of water, always watch your child at all times. Also, keep a close eye on teething toddlers who may decide a rock or leaf of poison oak is an interesting item to put in their mouth.

From spring through fall, you'll want your kids to wear a wide-brimmed hat to keep their face, head, and ears protected from the hot sun. Also, make sure your children wear sunscreen at all times. Choose a brand without PABA—children have sensitive skin and may have an allergic reaction to sunscreen that contains PABA. If you are hiking with a child younger than six months, don't use sunscreen or insect repellent. Instead, be sure that their head, face, neck, and ears are protected from the sun with a wide-brimmed hat, and that all other skin exposed to the sun is protected with the appropriate clothing.

Remember that food is fun. Kids like snacks, so it's important to bring a lot of munchies for the trail. Stopping often for snack breaks is a fun way to keep the trail interesting. Raisins, apples, granola bars, crackers and cheese, cereal, and trail mix all make great snacks. If your child is old enough to carry their own backpack, fill it with treats before you leave. If your kids don't like drinking water, you can bring boxes of fruit juice.

Avoid poorly designed child-carrying packs—you don't want to break your back carrying your child. Most child-carrying backpacks designed to hold a 40-pound child will contain a large carrying pocket to hold diapers and other items. Some have an optional rain/sun hood.

Hiking with Your Dog

Bringing your furry friend with you is always more fun than leaving him behind. Our canine pals make great trail buddies because they never complain and always make good company. Hiking with your dog can be a rewarding experience, especially if you plan ahead. Keep in mind, however, that dogs and archaeology don't mix. If you are hiking in an area where dogs are allowed, be sure to keep your companion leashed and away from any cultural sites to prevent digging and erosion. And it goes without saying that your dog's waste should be packed out just like your own.

Dogs & Archaeology Don't Mix

Getting your dog in shape. Before you plan outdoor adventures with your dog, make sure he's in shape for the trail. Getting your dog into shape takes the same discipline as getting yourself into shape, but luckily, your dog can get in shape with you. Take your dog with you on your daily runs or walks. If there is a park near your house, throw a tennis ball or play Frisbee with your dog.

Swimming is also an excellent way to get your dog into shape. If there is a lake or river near where you live and your dog likes the water, have him retrieve a tennis ball or stick. Gradually build your dog's stamina up over a two- to three-month period. A good rule of thumb is to assume that your dog will travel twice as far as you will on the trail. If you plan on doing a 5-mile hike, be sure your dog is in shape for a 10-mile hike.

Training your dog for the trail. Before you go on your first hiking adventure with your dog, be sure he has a firm grasp on the basics of canine etiquette and behavior. Make sure he can sit, lie down, stay, and come. One of the most important commands you can teach your canine pal is to "come" under any situation. It's easy for your friend's nose to lead him astray or possibly get lost. Another helpful command is the "get behind" command. When you're on a hiking trail that's narrow, you can have your dog follow behind you when other trail users approach. Nothing is more bothersome than an enthusiastic dog that runs back and forth on the trail and disrupts the peace of the trail for others. When you see other trail users approaching you on the trail, give them the right of way by quietly stepping off the trail and making your dog lie down and stay until they pass.

Equipment. The most critical pieces of equipment you can invest in for your dog are proper identification and a sturdy leash. Flexi-leads work well for hiking because they give your dog more freedom to explore but still leave you in control. Make sure your dog has identification that includes your name and address and a number for your veterinarian. Other forms of identification for your dog include a tattoo or a microchip. You should consult your veterinarian for more information on these last two options.

The next piece of equipment you'll want to consider is a pack for your dog. By no means should you hold all of your dog's essentials in your pack—let him carry his own gear! Dogs that are in good shape can carry 30 to 40 percent of their own weight.

Most packs are fitted by a dog's weight and girth measurement. Companies that make dog packs generally include guidelines to help you pick out the size that's right for your dog. Some characteristics to look for when purchasing a pack for your dog include a harness that contains two padded girth straps, a padded chest strap, leash attachments, removable saddle bags, internal water bladders, and external gear cords.

You can introduce your dog to the pack by first placing the empty pack on his back and letting him wear it around the yard. Keep an eye on him during this first introduction. He may decide to chew through the straps if you aren't watching him closely. Once he learns to treat the pack as an object of fun and not a foreign enemy, fill the pack evenly on both sides with a few ounces of dog food in resealable plastic bags. Have your dog wear his pack on your daily walks for a period of two to three weeks. Each week add a little more weight to the pack until your dog will accept carrying the maximum amount of weight he can carry.

You can also purchase collapsible water and dog food bowls for your dog. These bowls are lightweight and can easily be stashed into your pack or your dog's. If you are hiking on rocky terrain or in the snow, you can purchase footwear for your dog that will protect his feet from cuts and bruises.

Always carry plastic bags to remove feces from the trail. It is a courtesy to other trail users and helps protect local wildlife.

The following is a list of items to bring when you take your dog hiking: collapsible water bowls, a comb, a collar and a leash, dog food, plastic bags for feces, a dog pack, flea/tick powder, paw protection, water, and a first-aid kit that contains eye ointment, tweezers, scissors, stretchy foot wrap, gauze, antibacterial wash, sterile cotton-tip applicators, triple-antibiotic ointment, and cotton wrap.

First aid for your dog. Your dog is just as prone—if not more prone—to getting in trouble on the trail as you are, so be prepared. Here's a rundown of the more likely misfortunes that might befall your little friend.

Bees and wasps. If a bee or wasp stings your dog, remove the stinger with a pair of tweezers and place a mudpack or a cloth dipped in cold water over the affected area.

Porcupines. One good reason to keep your dog on a leash is to prevent him from getting a nose full of porcupine quills. You may be able to remove the quills with pliers, but a veterinarian is the best person to do this nasty job because most dogs need to be sedated.

Heatstroke. Avoid hiking with your dog in really hot weather. Dogs with heatstroke will pant excessively, lie down and refuse to get up, and become lethargic and disoriented. If your dog shows any of these signs on the trail, have him lie down in the shade. If you are near a stream, pour cool water over your dog's entire body to help bring his body temperature back to normal.

Heartworm. Dogs get heartworms from mosquitoes, which carry the disease in the prime mosquito months of July and August. Giving your dog a monthly pill prescribed by your veterinarian easily prevents this condition.

Plant pitfalls. One of the biggest plant hazards for dogs on the trail are foxtails. Foxtails are pointed grass seed heads that bury themselves in your friend's fur, between his toes, and even in his ear canal. If left unattended, these nasty seeds can work their way under the skin and cause abscesses and other problems. If you have a long-haired dog, consider trimming the hair between his toes and giving him a summer haircut to help prevent foxtails from attaching to his fur. After every hike, always look over your dog for these seeds—especially between his toes and his ears.

Other plant hazards include burrs, thorns, thistles, and poison oak. If you find any burrs or thistles on your dog, remove them as soon as possible before they become an unmanageable mat. Thorns can pierce a dog's foot and cause a great deal of pain. If you see that your dog is lame, stop and check his feet for thorns. Dogs are immune to poison oak, but they can pick up the sticky, oily substance from the plant and transfer it to you.

Protect those paws. Be sure to keep your dog's nails trimmed so he avoids getting soft tissue or joint injuries. If your dog slows and refuses to go on, check to see that his paws aren't torn or worn. You can protect your dog's paws from trail hazards such as sharp gravel, foxtails, lava scree, and thorns by purchasing dog boots.

Sunburn. If your dog has light skin he is an easy target for sunburn on his nose and other exposed skin areas. You can apply a nontoxic sunscreen to exposed skin areas that will help protect him from over-exposure to the sun.

Ticks and fleas. Ticks can easily give your dog Lyme disease, as well as other diseases. Before you hit the trail, treat your dog with a flea and tick spray or powder. You can also ask your veterinarian about a once-a-month pour-on treatment that repels fleas and ticks.

Mosquitoes and deer flies. These little flying machines can do a job on your dog's snout and ears. Best bet is to spray your dog with fly repellent for horses to discourage both pests.

Giardia. Dogs can get giardia, which results in diarrhea. It is usually not debilitating, but it's definitely messy. A vaccine against giardia is available.

Mushrooms. Make sure your dog doesn't sample mushrooms along the trail. They could be poisonous to him, but he doesn't know that.

When you are finally ready to hit the trail with your dog, keep in mind that national parks and many wilderness areas do not allow dogs on trails. Your best bet is to hike in national forests, BLM lands, and state parks. Always call ahead or check the website to see what the restrictions are.

Further Reading

The American Southwest has inspired a lifetime's worth of literature. Here is an introductory collection of works that highlight some of the beauty, challenge, and drama of this singular landscape, both around Bears Ears and across the Colorado Plateau.

Archaeology and History

Anasazi America: Seventeen Centuries on the Road from Center Place by David E. Stuart. (University of New Mexico Press, 2000).

The Chaco Meridian: Centers of Political Power in the Ancient Southwest by Stephen H. Lekson. (AltaMira Press, 1999).

Cliff Dwellers of Cedar Mesa: The Culture, Sites, and Exodus of the Ancestral Puebloans by Donald J. Rommes and William D. Lipe. (Canyonlands Natural History Association, 2013).

Cowboys & Cave Dwellers: Basketmaker Archaeology in Utah's Grand Gulch by Fred M. Blackburn and Ray A. Williamson. (School of American Research Press, 1997).

Legacy on Stone: Rock Art of the Colorado Plateau and Four Corners Region by Sally J. Cole. (Johnson Books, 2009).

Artifact Trafficking

Finders Keepers: A Tale of Archaeological Plunder and Obsession by Craig Childs. (Back Bay Books, 2013).

Plunder of the Ancients: A True Story of Betrayal, Redemption, and an Undercover Quest to Recover Sacred Native American Artifacts by Lucinda Delaney Schroeder. (Lyons Press, 2014).

Plundered Skulls and Stolen Spirits: Inside the Fight to Reclaim Native America's Culture by Chip Colwell. (University of Chicago Press, 2017).

Fiction

Hunting Badger by Tony Hillerman. (Harper, 2010).

The Monkey Wrench Gang by Edward Abbey. (Lippincott, 1975).

Natural History

Wind in the Rock: The Canyonlands of Southeastern Utah by Ann Zwinger. (University of Arizona Press, 1986).

Personal Narrative

Cities of Gold: A Journey Across the American Southwest by Douglas Preston. (University of New Mexico Press, 1999).

Desert Solitaire: A Season in the Wilderness by Edward Abbey. (Ballantine Books, 1971).

House of Rain: Tracking a Vanished Civilization Across the American Southwest by Craig Childs. (Back Bay Books, 2008).

In Search of the Old Ones: Exploring the Anasazi World of the Southwest by David Roberts. (Simon & Schuster, 1997).

The Lost World of the Old Ones: Discoveries in the Ancient Southwest by David Roberts. (W.W. Norton & Co., 2016).

Water and Land-Use Issues

The Colorado River: Flowing Through Conflict by Peter McBride and Jonathan Waterman. (Westcliffe Publishers, 2010).

A Great Aridness: Climate Change and the Future of the American Southwest by William deBuys. (Oxford University Press, 2010).

Roads in the Wilderness: Conflict in Canyon Country by Jedediah S. Rogers. (University of Utah Press, 2013).

Voices from Bears Ears: Seeking Common Ground on Sacred Land by Rebecca M. Robinson. (University of Arizona Press, 2018).

Where the Water Goes: Life and Death Along the Colorado River by David Owen. (Riverhead Books, 2017).

Glossary of Terms

Anasazi: A now-outdated term for the people who first populated Bears Ears and left the **rock art** and decaying structures we still see today. Replaced by **Ancestral Puebloans**.

Ancestral Puebloans: The current preferred term for the first peoples to populate Bears Ears, emphasizing that today's Puebloan Native Americans are their descendants. The best-known modern Puebloans include the Hopi, Zuni, Taos, and Acoma peoples.

Ancients: A general term to refer to the **Ancestral Puebloans** or any other groups who left traces of themselves in the Bears Ears region in the distant past. "We were walking in the footsteps of the ancients."

Anthropomorph: A **rock art** figure whose shape, form, or profile suggests a human being, or humanoid.

Archaeology: The scientific study of human history and prehistory through the recovery and analysis of physical evidence, including artifacts and remains. Also used as a general term for ancient ruins or **rock art**, as in "That canyon was full of archaeology."

Atlatl: A tool used to increase leverage and velocity in spear throwing. Essentially a stick that allows a spear to be attached at the end, effectively increasing the length of the user's throwing arm.

BCE: Before the Common Era, a replacement for the BC year designation; 1,000 BCE and 1,000 BC refer to the same year.

BLM: Bureau of Land Management, a federal government agency that owns and manages much of the public land throughout the western United States.

Butte: An isolated hill or high point with steep sides and a flat top, generally narrower than a **mesa**. Buttes are often taller than they are wide, but that is not a requirement. The Bears Ears Buttes do not match this definition, for example.

Cairn: A pile of rocks or stones used to mark a route where a trail is difficult to follow or altogether nonexistent. Although you may frequently find cairns in the backcountry that are helpful in showing you the way, please refrain from building any new ones.

CE: Common Era, a replacement for the AD year designation; AD 1956 and 1956 CE refer to the same year.

Chaco: A general term that can refer to Chaco Canyon in New Mexico, the large civilization built there and then abandoned by the **Ancestral Puebloans** circa 1300 CE, or the remains of the large structures ("great houses") still standing there today, as featured in Chaco Culture National Historical Park. Often used in reference to the vast influence the Chaco culture exerted on its neighbors, as in "This kiva is built in a Chacoan style."

Friction pitch: A sometimes-steep section of a trail or route that requires hiking directly up an exposed **slickrock** face, so-named because a successful ascent depends on the friction between the sole of your shoe and the rock.

GCNRA: Glen Canyon National Recreation Area.

Ghost wall: A wall that has disappeared from a ruin site but whose prior existence is indicated by an outline left on a rock face or on a still-standing structure.

Hoodoo: A tall, thin tower or spire of rock.

Jacal: An early building style featuring walls made of poles or sticks covered with mud or clay.

Kachina: A spirit being from the Puebloan Native American religious tradition. Can also refer to a doll, figure, or human ceremonial dancer representing the spirit being.

KGRS: Kane Gulch Ranger Station.

Kiva: An underground ceremonial chamber used by both **Ancestral Puebloans** and their modern descendants. Access is typically down a wooden ladder through a hole in the roof. Most kivas in the Bears Ears region were built in the circular Mesa Verde style, but some show the square Kayenta style instead. Sometimes built aboveground in places where excavation into hard bedrock is impossible, such as on sandstone ledges or shelves.

Mano: A smooth, handheld stone used in conjunction with a **metate** to grind seeds, grain, and other basic foods, especially maize (corn).

Meander: A winding curve or bend in a river or canyon.

Mesa: A raised area of land with steep sides and a flat top, generally broader than a **butte**. Borrowed from the Spanish word for "table," mesas are small plateaus and are generally much wider than they are high.

Metate: A smooth stone used as a base for grinding food in conjunction with a **mano**. Typically a hollowed-out, bowl-like depression worn into the upper surface of a rock.

Midden: An old pile of refuse and discarded items; an ancient trash heap, usually of great interest to archaeologists due to its high concentration of artifacts. Although a midden can be difficult to identify in the field, it is usually a mound located at the front of a ruin with darker soil than its surroundings. Middens should be avoided and left undisturbed.

Oxbow: A horseshoe-shaped bend in a river or canyon, usually deeper than a **meander**.

Petroglyph: In **rock art**, a figure or image that is pecked, incised, or carved directly into the surface of the rock.

Pictograph: In **rock art**, a figure or image that is painted onto the surface of the rock, using any of a number of natural adhesive pigments and colors.

Pithouse: A simple dwelling dug into the ground. A likely precursor to a **kiva**.

Pour-off: A dry waterfall, often presenting a significant obstacle to travel up or down a canyon. May suddenly come to life during a flash flood.

Rincon: From the Spanish word for "corner," an abandoned **meander** of a river. Created when the main channel of a river erodes through a canyon wall to shortcut an **oxbow** bend.

Rock art or Rock imagery: Human-made drawings, paintings, or markings on natural stone surfaces, generally ancient or prehistoric. Typically found as either **petroglyphs** or **pictographs**.

Sipapu: A small hole or hollow in the floor of a **kiva** or **pithouse**. Also the term for the portal that the spiritual ancestors of the Puebloan people are believed to have passed through to first emerge into the present world, which the hole in the floor symbolizes.

Slickrock: An area of exposed sandstone. The name was used by early European settlers because the sandstone offered low traction for their horses' metal shoes, especially when wet, but slickrock generally offers good traction for modern rubber soles.

Slide: Short for rockslide, often the main access route in and out of a canyon. "We had to descend the slide to reach the canyon floor."

Superimposition: In **rock art**, the placing of newer images directly on top of older ones.

USFS: United States Forest Service.

USGS: United States Geological Survey.

Wash: A dry riverbed or creek bed. May suddenly come to life during a flash flood.

Zoomorph: A **rock art** figure whose shape, form, or profile suggests an animal, like a deer or a bighorn sheep. Can also refer to figures that portray humans or deities as animals or as having animal-like qualities.

Acknowledgments

The first time I stepped into a Cedar Mesa canyon I was already working on this book, although no one knew it at the time–especially not me. Thanks to everyone who's ever spent a day with me in the canyons over the years, including Dan Brady, Soren Bowie, Damian Costello, and Eric Barth. I'm glad we got to share the adventure. Special thanks to Bryce Stevens, who was there right from the beginning and who's seen more of the canyon country with me than anyone. You never failed to remind me there's always a way, even when the route is hidden.

I owe a particular debt of gratitude to Laura Lantz and Scott Edwards at Kane Gulch for giving me the opportunity to work as a volunteer ranger all those years ago. It's not everyone's ambition to live in a trailer without running water in the middle of nowhere, but it's something I'll never forget. Along with the entire staff of the BLM Monticello Field Office, you showed me how to serve something bigger than myself and what real dedication can achieve, despite a lack of resources, support, or funds. You were the very image of professionalism in the face of impossible circumstances.

Without Friends of Cedar Mesa, I would never have been involved in this project at all. Thanks to Josh Ewing, Amanda Podmore, Erica Tucker, and Stephanie Wacha for first recruiting me as an author and then answering all of my endless requests for materials and assistance. If this book helps your organization achieve any of its goals, I will consider it a runaway success.

Lastly, thanks to the entire crew at FalconGuides for shepherding this project across the finish line and launching it into the world. In particular, I couldn't have done it without my invaluable editors, Jess d'Arbonne, Katie O'Dell, and Lynn Zelem, who kept me on the trail when it would have been so easy to get lost in rock formations along the way.

Despite all the assistance I have received, any errors in the final copy are my responsibility alone. Additionally, although Friends of Cedar Mesa was involved in many aspects of the creation of this book, they did not review the text and are not responsible for any of its content.

About the Author

Starting with a life-changing trip to Cedar Mesa in the fall of 2001, Andrew Weber has spent two decades exploring the landscape and archaeology of the Four Corners region, including several years as a volunteer ranger at Kane Gulch. He has also worked at Mesa Verde National Park, helping to digitize the park's archaeological records, and served as an archaeological site steward in Canyons of the Ancients National Monument.

Andrew Weber

Working as a freelance journalist and photographer, Andrew has written about a wide range of topics, including cultural events, the arts, and professional sports. This is his third guidebook, after *60 Hikes Within 60 Miles: Seattle* and *Easy Hikes Close to Home: Seattle*.

He currently resides on the Navajo Nation in the town of Shiprock, New Mexico, with his wife and two sons.